Copyright © 2002
Morning Sun Books, Inc.

All rights reserved. This book may not be reproduced in part or in whole without written permission from the publisher, except in the case of brief quotations or reproductions of the cover for the purposes of review.

To access our full library *In Color* visit us at
www.morningsunbooks.com

ROBERT J. YANOSEY, President

Published by
Morning Sun Books, Inc.
9 Pheasant Lane
Scotch Plains, NJ 07076
Printed in Korea

Library of Congress
Catalog Card No. 2002103683

First Printing
ISBN 1-58248-078-8

DEDICATION

Monon in Color
is dedicated
to the memory of:

JOSEPH LEWNARD

Dining Car Steward and Chef

Chicago, Indianapolis
and Louisville

and

CAROLINE BENTON LEWNARD

The first woman
Dining Car Steward
Cincinnati, Hamilton,
and Dayton

ACKNOWLEDGMENTS

This book would not be possible without the kind and gracious assistance of the following people. Thanks go to:

- Edward Lewnard, editor of *The Hoosier Line* for many years, who took us on many excursions to South Hammond and Lafayette to see the Monon. He inspired us with stories of riding the Monon dining cars with Grandpa Joe over the years, and provided many of the documents needed to verify the information in the captions.

- Owen Leander, photographer and good friend, who suggested that I write this book and provided the many pictures that, appear throughout its pages.

- Joseph Lewnard, who helped edit the pictures and the text.

- Richard Baldwin, who welcomed me into his home and spent hours explaining the operations of the Monon on the Indianapolis Line. Richard also provided a large number of pictures for this book.

- Tom Smart, who took the majority of the photographs south of McDoel Yard.

- To the following photographers who generously shared their photographic work: Richard Baldwin, Melvern Finzer, John Fuller, Sanford Goodrick, John Hanacek, Matthew Herson, J. David Ingles, Owen Leander, Edward Lewnard, Joseph Lewnard, Russell F. Munroe, Michael Sink, Dr. James W. Smith, Lewis Unnewehr, Richard Wallin, and Robert Zelisko.

- Dan and Tom Anthony, who helped pick up and deliver slides in Indiana.

- Robert J. Yanosey, who guided me through this project and located a number of the slides in this book.

- Special thanks also goes to the many members of the Monon Historical Society who provided support and encouragement for this project. Many details of the captions were checked for accuracy with Monon Railroad documents that were graciously provided by the Society.

MONON In Color

The Monon on the Chicago and Western Indiana	7
The First Sub-division:	
State Line Tower to Shops Yard	19
The Fourth Sub-division:	
Shops Yard to McDoel	42
The Fifth Sub-division:	
McDoel to Youngstown Yard	50
The Second Sub-division:	
Monon to Indianapolis	77
The Third Sub-division:	
Michigan City to Monon and the French Lick Branch	87
The Diesel Fleet	96
The Freight Car Fleet	108
The Passenger Car Fleet	116
Cabooses and Work Equipment	124

ABOVE • An F3a is serviced at the Belt Jct. Roundhouse in Indianapolis in April of 1959. *(Richard Baldwin)*

MONON

THE HOOSIER LINE

THE MONON WAS A COLORFUL, FASCINATING RAILROAD TO WATCH. Its diesel fleet was unique, its color schemes attractive, and its operations were understandable. On an average day in the 1960's the Monon ran two passenger trains, eight to ten road freights and eight locals. There were also the Chicago area transfers and the many local switch jobs in the cities that the Monon served. Monon had a variety of interesting diesels that were not commonly seen on other Indiana railroads, such as BL2's and C420's.

The focus of this book is to explain the operations of the Monon in the time period from 1947 to 1971. It intentionally avoids the historical approach taken by the two well written histories of the Monon: *The Monon Route*, by George W. Hilton and *Monon, The Hoosier Line*, by Gary W. Dolzall and Stephen F. Dolzall. Instead, *Monon in Color* will explore the operations of the freight and passenger trains, the assignment of the crews, the blocking of the trains, and the operations of the transfer and switch crews. Exploration of the Monon begins at Dearborn Station in Chicago and runs south to Youngstown Yard in Louisville. Picking up again at Monon, the book examines the Indianapolis and Michigan City lines. Then it takes a brief look at the diesels and equipment of the Monon.

Most of the information in this book came from Monon Railroad documents, including: employee timetables, *The Information Book for the Inspection Trip on the Monon of 1951*, Monon Equipment Diagrams, Monon dispatchers train sheets from 1954 to 1971, Monon Railroad documents explaining crew assignments, yard jobs and transfers, as well as timebooks of retired Monon railroad employees. The Monon Historical Technical Society produces an excellent magazine entitled *The Hoosier Line* that is published three times a year. Over the years the Society has published several volumes of useful information. Also, Montford Switzer has authored a large number of articles on Monon diesels and freight equipment that has been published both in *Mainline Modeler* and in *Railroad Model Craftsman*.

Any mistakes in the text or the interpretation are solely the author's responsibility. Readers are invited to share their insights to help assemble a more accurate historical record of the operations of the Monon.

ABOVE • Many Monon crossings were protected by this unique device that was displayed in addition to the normal wooden crossbucks. When the right of way was clear the green light was displayed. As a train approached the light went out, and motorists were warned by the sign : "Danger, when the light is out cross at your own risk."
(Richard Baldwin)

BELOW • Monon C420 502 leads #5, THE THOROUGHBRED at Hammond in September of 1967. (Richard Wallin)

MONON In Color

The Monon Railroad in the Modern Era · 1946-1971

A POWERFUL ENTHUSIASM FILLED THE HEARTS and minds of John Barriger's management team when it took over control of the Chicago, Indianapolis, and Louisville Railroad, (more commonly known as the Monon), on May 1st, 1946. Like many other railroaders in the years following the defeat of the Axis powers in WWII, they were convinced that the success in the future belonged to the railroad that could provide fast, efficient, and reliable service to its shippers and passengers. Success to John Barriger meant modern, efficient, diesel-powered passenger trains running with streamlined equipment on fast, frequent schedules. Success meant diesel-powered freights that ran on reliable schedules that a shipper could count on. Success meant that the railroad had to be rebuilt to eliminate ancient bridges, excessive curvature, and an antiquated right of way that too often ran in the middle of city streets. Success meant that the CI&L's outdated motive power and freight cars had to be replaced. And of course, success meant that the railroad had to spend huge amounts of money that it just didn't have.

So Barriger and his assistants did as much as they could with the resources that were available. Purchasing a small fleet of diesels, they eliminated steam engines, coaling towers, water plugs, and unneeded engine houses in three years. When they couldn't obtain the passenger cars they needed from the major builders, they rebuilt U.S. Army hospital cars into beautiful red and gray streamliners. They doubled the number of passenger trains and speeded them up. They provided the U.S. Post Office and the Railway Express Agency modern, efficient postal cars and baggage cars. Somehow they found enough cash to almost completely replace the aged freight car fleet. Depots and bridges were rebuilt, repainted, or replaced. They even rerouted a few miles of mainline out of a swamp.

The Monon Railroad that Barriger and his team renewed and in a sense recreated was resourceful, efficient and proud. Employee morale rose significantly. Trains ran on time. Brightly colored red and gray streamliners connected Chicago with Indianapolis, Louisville, and points in between. Black and gold powered freights ran three times a day on the mainline and daily on the Michigan City and Indianapolis lines. Local freights provided service to customers every day but Sunday. The Lafayette Shops hummed with activity, building passenger cars and cabooses, renewing diesels, and creating ingenious adaptations that made the freight car fleet well suited to the shippers needs.

The railroad they ran was well suited to the 1950's, but it suffered several severe limitations that even John Barriger knew limited the Monon's future. He knew that the Monon was too dependent upon coal, grain and stone. He knew that Monon served too many small towns in rural Indiana, and that it lacked adequate access to major sources of traffic in the big cities that it served, especially in Indianapolis. Even as he rebuilt Indiana's own railroad, Barriger knew that success meant that Monon had to be merged with or sold to another railroad. So ultimately and perhaps unknowingly, John Barriger and his successors prepared the Monon for its eventual merger with the Louisville and Nashville RR in July of 1971.

The Monon of 1946-1971 was one of the oldest railroads in the state of Indiana. On the map of Indiana the Monon formed a large X that crossed the whole western part of the state with two major lines that intersected in the small city of Monon. The original stem of the Chicago, Indianapolis, and Louisville was built as the New Albany and Salem, which constructed the mainline that ultimately extended from New Albany on the Ohio River to Michigan City on Lake Michigan in 1847-1854. The New Albany line was renamed the New Albany, Louisville and Chicago. The New Albany later gained control of and completed the Indianapolis, Delphi & Chicago, which had begun the construction of the Chicago to Indianapolis mail line in 1880. Unfortunately for the Monon, the decision to build to Michigan City rather than Chicago would place it at a serious disadvantage in later years. The railroad was renamed the Chicago, Indianapolis, and Louisville after a bankruptcy in 1896.

The Monon was unusual in that it had very few branch lines. The two branch lines that were operated in the 1946-1971 era were the French Lick and Midland branches. The Orleans to French Lick branch was built in 1880 and the Wallace Jct. to Midland (Victoria) branch was built in 1906. Monon was also unusual in that all of the trackage that it owned was totally in the state of Indiana. The Monon entered Chicago over the tracks of the Chicago and Western Indiana and entered Louisville over the tracks of the Kentucky and Indiana Terminal. Although it had its own yard in Indianapolis, the Monon accessed the passenger terminal and its principal connections via the Indianapolis Union Ry.

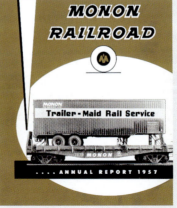

Monon Operations

The post-WWII Monon was a small but efficient operation that provided excellent service to its passengers and shippers. The Monon owned 512.25 miles of mainline and branches, which meant that the whole railroad was just about the size of a division on a major railroad. For many years one dispatcher located in Lafayette could record the movement of all the trains that ran each day on just one train sheet. The Monon operated its trains into Chicago on 19.82 miles of the Chicago and Western Indiana, of which it was 20% owner. Monon transfers ran on the Belt Railway of Chicago mainline to Clearing Yard in the center of Chicago. Monon owned 1/12th of the BRC. Access to Louisville was via 6.17 miles of the Kentucky and Indiana Terminal, which the Monon jointly owned with the Baltimore and Ohio and the Southern. Monon passenger trains continued on to Louisville's Union Station via 1.10 miles of the Louisville and Nashville. Entry into Indianapolis was gained via 1.07 miles of trackage rights on the Nickel Plate and Big Four, as well as .69 miles of operation on the Indianapolis Union.

For operational purposes the Monon was divided into seven sub-divisions. The Barriger management devised an operating plan that was adhered to with minor variations from 1947 until 1960, when changing traffic patterns and rising costs made train consolidations necessary. Barriger's idea was to run relatively short, fast freights on reliable schedules. Since Indiana law required an extra brakeman on all trains longer than 70 cars, there was an added incentive to run smaller trains. Three freights trains numbered #70-75 ran each way from to South Hammond to K&IT's Youngstown Yard in Louisville on 10-12 hour schedules. In theory a car received from the Belt Ry. at Clearing Yard in Chicago at 3PM could be delivered to the K&IT Youngstown Yard in Louisville by 7AM the next morning. The 70 series freights were supplemented by trains #56-57 running from Michigan City to Lafayette and #90-91 running from Monon to Belt Jct. in Indianapolis.

Dispatchers train sheets from the period indicate that the Monon consistently delivered the freight within the schedule day after day. In addition, each sub-division had one or two scheduled locals numbered in the 40 series to serve local industries. These locals ran daily except Sunday. The locals ran in the daytime delivering and gathering cars that were relayed to the time freights at South Hammond, Monon, Lafayette, and McDoel Yard in Bloomington. Cars picked up by the locals were usually delivered to connecting railroads within 24 hours.

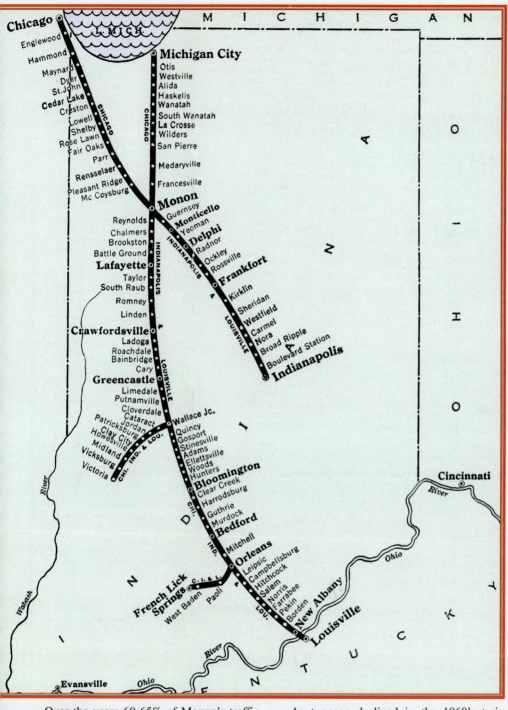

al observer might think that there were no trains on the Monon at all. During the day a local might pass, or one might catch a glimpse of #6, THE THOROUGHBRED, pausing at a station. But if one stood on the platform of the Monon depot from 11PM until 3AM he/she would see a procession of trains as #70-71,56-57, and 90/91 exchanged cars in the two adjacent yards. During the day most of the activity was in Hammond, Michigan City, and Indianapolis, as the switch engines broke the road freights apart and the transfers made their deliveries.

South of Lafayette the pattern was the opposite. Trains #70-73 could be found on the Fourth and Fifth Sub-divisions in daylight. THE THOROUGHBRED left Louisville at dawn and spent most of the morning heading north to Chicago. McDoel Yard hummed with activity as it dispatched three or four locals and the road freights picked up and set out cars.

Over the years certain cities became the focal points for Monon's operations. The operational heart of the Monon was Lafayette. Located at milepost 117.9 in Lafayette was Shops. At Shops the Monon repaired and renewed its locomotives and cars. The dispatching and operating offices were also located in Lafayette. A large yard ran parallel to Shops where road freights were serviced and trains were reblocked. At the north end of the system was South Hammond yard, where all of the 70 series freights as well as the transfers into Chicago were assembled or broken down. At the center of the railroad's X sat Monon, where the Chicago to Indianapolis line crossed the New Albany to Louisville line. (The railroad considered the Chicago to Louisville trackage to be the mainline. The Michigan City and Indianapolis lines were considered branches.) As many as 15 freight trains passed through or exchanged cars at Monon each day. Michigan City and Indianapolis both had important yards. On the south end McDoel Yard played a critical role in keeping the railroad fluid. In addition to the facilities located at Shops, there were roundhouses at South Hammond, Belt Jct., and McDoel.

Monon's postwar operations were simple and efficient. From 1946 until 1949 Monon provided overnight trains #3-4, THE NIGHT EXPRESS / BLUEGRASS, on the Chicago to Louisville line with connections to French Lick via trains #23/24. Pullman service was provided to Louisville and French Lick. On the day run to Louisville the Monon ran #5-6, THE THOROUGHBRED. Dining and parlor car service was provided on #5/6 from 1948 until 1951. A grille coach then ran until 1956, when THE THOROUGHBRED became coach only. THE THOROUGHBRED was discontinued on September 30, 1967. Both of the Louisville trains provided railway postal service until the RPO cars were withdrawn in December of 1965. Monon provided double daily passenger service from Chicago to Indianapolis until April 10th, 1959. Trains #11-12, THE TIPPECANOE, and #14-15, THE HOOSIER, provided coach, dining and parlor service until 1957. Both of these trains also had RPO cars for U.S. mail service. The two trains then briefly ran

Over the years 60-65% of Monon's traffic was received from connecting lines. A considerable portion of this freight was bridge traffic being relayed to other connecting railroads. One might expect that most of this traffic would run from Louisville or Indianapolis to Chicago. But the Monon also received and delivered blocks of cars from rural connections such as the Southern at French Lick or the Nickel Plate at Linden for delivery to other railroads. A lively interchange took place with the Milwaukee Road at Bedford, the Pennsylvania at Gosport, and the Wabash at Lafayette. Since the Michigan City line intersected all of the major railroads entering Chicago from the east, it was possible to deliver eastbound connecting traffic without the encountering the problems inherent in the complexity of the Chicago Terminal District.

As tonnage declined in the 1960's train operations were modified so that there were fewer, longer trains. Trains #70-71 continued to run from South Hammond to Louisville. #73-73 ran daily south of Lafayette and four days a week north of Lafayette. #74-75 were discontinued. #56/57 and #90-91 ran as usual, but the locals were modified so that each mainline subdivision had one local running north three days a week and south three days a week. The locals on the Michigan City line ran as a turn from Monon to Wilders, and the Indianapolis local ran from Monon to Monticello. These trains were supplemented by locals operating in the Bloomington-Bedford stone district and extras operating on the French Lick and Midland branches.

The Monon of the 1960's had an interesting operating pattern. North of Lafayette almost all of the freight trains ran in darkness, arriving at their terminals in the early morning. A casu-

5

with only RPO and express cars until the mail contract expired later that month. Monon also ran many special trains over the years. The most notable of these trains were the Derby Day Specials and the many Football Specials for Purdue and Indiana games. The Monon also hosted Metropolitan Opera Specials and KofC specials. Unlike its neighbors NYC and PRR, the Monon never really had enough mail and express business to run solid mail trains.

The Monon was one of the first railroads in the United States to be completely dieselized. Dieselization actually began during WWII when the Monon acquired an SW1 and 3 NW2's from EMD. To power of all of the trains the Barriger administration purchased more units so that by 1949 the fleet included 10 passenger F3's, 17 freight F3's, 20 roadswitchers, and 20 switch engines. Sample rosters appear below. Although three F3's had to be replaced in 1948 because of the wreck at Ash Grove, the diesel fleet remained essentially intact until 1963. There was a brief flirtation with six-axle C628's that resulted in the units being sold to the Lehigh Valley after four years in service. As the fleet wore out, Monon rebuilt nine RS2's and acquired 18 C420's and 8 U23b's to replace the aging F units and BL2's. Unlike most railroads at the time, the Monon was not impressed with EMD's GP and SD units, remaining loyal to Alco until the builder left the business in 1969.

The Monon railroad that merged with the L&N in July of 1971 remained a success. It provided good service to its many customers with pride and efficiency. The Monon's employees were dedicated, hard working, and friendly and the road was in good shape. The merger proved to be well timed. It is doubtful that the Monon could have survived in the modern era, given the growing strength of long haul trucks using the Interstate Highway system and the consolidation of the major railroads into a few systems. It was simply too small to survive as a regional railroad. It lost a considerable portion of its coal business in the 1960's and the realignment of traffic patterns after the creation of Conrail would have left it extremely vulnerable. Most of Monon's interchange points are no longer used. The simple fact is that railroading today is not conducted the way the Monon was run.

The core of the Monon still exists under the ownership of the CSX Corporation, but operations have been significantly modified. Trains no longer run north of Dyer. The mainline north of Dyer, South Hammond Yard and the C&WI mainline to Pullman Jct. have been abandoned. The Michigan City line terminates at Medaryville and the Indianapolis line is abandoned south of Monticello. Amtrak trains and CSX freight still run between Dyer and Ames or Greencastle, but the mainline is broken from south of Greencastle to Mitchell. CSX freight trains still run south of Mitchell, and Canadian Pacific freights run south from Bedford to Louisville. The Midland and French Lick branches were also abandoned.

Roster of Monon Diesels December 1949

Number	Type	Year Built
5-6	SW1	1949
11-17	NW2	1942, 1947
18	H10-44	1946
21-29	RS2	1947
30-38	BL2	1948-1949
45-46	H15-44	1947
51A&B	F3a	1946,19477
61A&B-65A&B	F3a	1946-1948
61C-65C	F3b	1946-1947
81A&B-85A&B	F3a	1947

Roster of Monon Diesels December 1964

Number	Type	Year Built	
11-17	NW2	1942, 1947	
21-29	RS2	1947	
30-38	BL2	1948-1949	
45-46	H15-44	1947	
101-112	F3a	1946-1948	freight F units
201-210	F3a	1947	
301—305	F3b	1946-1947	
400-408	C628	1964	

Monon Railroad records are not always clear as to when a unit was retired. It is likely that several of the 100 and 300 series F units were out of service or scrapped by December of 1964. They are listed here to show the whole roster with clarity.

Roster of Monon Diesels June 1971

Number	Type	Year Built	
12-13, 15-17	NW2	1942, 1947	
32	BL2	1948	
51-59	RS2	1947	
203, 204, 209	F3a	1947	passenger F units
501-502	C420	1966	passenger units
503-518	C420	1966-1967	freight units
601-608	U23b	1970	

ABOVE • Monon RS2 56 at South Hammond Yard, November 26, 1965. (Roger Puta, Mel Finzer collection)

MONON

Monon Operations on the Chicago and Western Indiana

THE HOOSIER LINE

ABOVE • At 5:25PM each day in from 1964 until 1967 Monon train #5, THE THOROUGHBRED, departed for Louisville from Dearborn Station, (also known as Polk St. Station). Owned and operated by the Chicago and Western Indiana RR, Dearborn is milepost zero for the Monon. Monon was one of five owners of the C&WI, which also included the Wabash, the Grand Trunk Western, the Chicago and Eastern Illinois, and the Erie. Santa Fe was a tenant. The C&WI maintained the terminal, switched the trains with its large fleet of RS1s, and serviced the passenger cars of its owners at the coach yard at 51st St. Monon passenger trains and transfers ran south on the double track C&WI mainline for 19.8 miles to State Line Interlocking, where Monon track ownership began. Today's version of #5 is lead by C420 501, which has been in service for just eleven months. Dearborn Station July 24, 1967.
(Tom Smart, Matthew Herson collection)

RIGHT • Deep inside the Dearborn station trainshed in 1959, F3a 84A prepares to haul a short, four car passenger train south. Dearborn's platforms were cold and drafty in the winter, and very hot in the summer. Countless passenger walked down the wooden platforms to entrain for far and exotic places. At the peak of its service in the years following WWII four Monon trains departed and arrived Dearborn each day. Two of these went to Indianapolis, and the other two went to Louisville. Monon's most exotic destination was the Kentucky Derby. Over the years long Derby specials departed Dearborn with as many as twenty Pullmans. But today the train is mundane, with mostly express and mail for points south. *(Paul C. Winters)*

Above • Shortly before Monon shifted THE THOROUGHBRED to an evening departure, RS2 23 leads #5 out of the train shed and under Roosevelt Road, which was also known as 12th St. The bi-directional RS2's were used between South Hammond and Dearborn station whenever one unit was sufficient to power #5 and #6. During the 1960's Monon did not want to pay the C&WI to turn the F3's at the roundhouse at 47th St. Passenger power was normally serviced at Lafayette Shops anyway, and there was only a short delay to the passengers trains when the units were exchanged at South Hammond. Dearborn Station, July 5, 1964. *(Owen Leander)*

Above • RS2 55 arrives at Dearborn with #6 at 2:00PM on September 16, 1967. THE THOROUGHBRED was rarely late in its final years of operation, which is remarkable given the fact that #6 had to pass through many complicated junctions between St. John's, Indiana and its final destination in Chicago. Since the two C420's 501 and 502 were the normal power for #5 and #6 by late 1967, it was rare for an RS2 to power the train. On this particular day the 55 brought the train north from Lafayette because 501 was on a freight and 502 was in the shop for servicing. *(Owen Leander)*

ABOVE • On July 5th, 1965 F3a 209 leads THE THOROUGHBRED south on another trip to Louisville. Sitting alongside are the RPO and express cars that came north on #6 earlier in the afternoon. Express and mail cars were normally set over to the east side of the depot in the Annex, where over ten tracks were available for loading and unloading. Since #6 arrived at 1:25PM and #5 departed at 5:25PM, there wasn't enough time to unload and reload the head end cars for the next southbound departure. When the train was turned in the station the last baggage car and coaches would normally be arranged to return south, but the RPO and express cars would stay in the terminal overnight. So even though only one train set was theoretically sufficient for daily operation, Monon maintained 3 RPO cars and 17 baggage and express cars, a fleet large enough to run three trains. *(Owen Leander)*

ABOVE • Sitting at the east side of Dearborn Station on September 2, 1967, C420 502 will be set over to #5 in a few minutes. It was very common to see Monon units lying over between trains in the depot, as the railroad tried to get the maximum mileage out of each unit every day. A single C420 was usually more than adequate for THE THOROUGHBRED by this point in time. The two passenger C420's were rarely used together on a passenger train. A typical service cycle would have 502 run the passengers for at least a week, after which it would be rotated with 501 at Lafayette Shops on a northbound run. The other C420 would then be used in freight and local service until the rotation was repeated again. *(Owen Leander)*

Above • Monon had long held the U.S. Post Office contract for operating Railway Post Office cars between Chicago and Louisville. Thus is came as a shock when the Post Office withdrew the RPO cars at the end of 1965. The RPO cars that operated after January 1st were assigned to storage mail service and sorting of the mail was no longer performed enroute. Monon tried to make up the loss carrying express for the Railway Express Agency. At times as many as five or six REA express cars would be at the head of the train. On July 3rd, 1966 #5 leaves Dearborn with one express car, a baggage, and two coaches. It will arrive at Louisville at 1:30AM the next morning. *(Matthew Herson)*

Above ◉ On a very cold December day in 1962 RS2 23 sits under the 12th St. bridge, its steam generator leaking a good amount of heat. The unit's 1500 H.P. will easily handle the four or five cars of #5 to South Hammond, where an F3a will take over the rest of the run. Six of Monon's nine RS2's were built with steam generators. Company records indicate that 23 did not have a steam generator or mu connections when it was built, but it is clear that this equipment was added at a later date. The RS2's had small fuel and water tanks, so Monon usually would not use them all the way from Chicago to Louisville. Monon's dispatchers train sheets show several occasions when RS2's substituted for the F3's or the C420's, but if they ran south of Hammond on a passenger train, they were almost always changed out at Lafayette for another set of power. *(Emery Gulash)*

Left ◉ After a Monon passenger train arrived at Dearborn, a CWI RS1 would couple on the rear, place the express and mail cars over to the house tracks and set the coaches out of the way until later in the day when #5 or #15 would be assembled. When the F3's were run back to back there was no need to take them to 47th St. to be turned, so they were also set out of the way until needed. The engines were normally serviced at Lafayette Shops. There was little need to fuel and water the units during the layover at Dearborn. F3a 204 was built by EMD as 82B in May of 1947, and it was renumbered to 204 in October of 1962. It was one of 4 F3'a (203, 204, 207, and 209) regularly used on #5 & 6 until the delivery of the C420's in 1966.

(J.W. Swanberg)

ABOVE • Until 1954 Monon maintained a freight house and a commissary west of the trainshed at Dearborn Station. For years dining car supplies that were kept in the commissary were delivered by cart across the wooden platforms to the trains after they were backed in from the coach yards. Although the passenger units would frequently be set aside near the commissary, they were rarely placed that far down into the terminal. In the late afternoon the 3:15PM crew from Hammond would arrive with an NW2 or a BL2 and a caboose. They would assemble the cars loaded at the freight house with merchandise, turn, and run quickly south to make a connection for #71. By the time F3a 210 sat waiting for its train on December 29, 1963 these operations had long passed. Monon switch runs no longer ran into the terminal, and dining car service had been discontinued in September of 1957. *(George Berisso)*

ABOVE • After passing under Roosevelt Road, the first interlocker encountered by a Monon train was at 15th St. where the C&WI connected with the Santa Fe coach yard leads. The GTW, C&EI and Wabash had freight houses at this location. Southbound trains used track #2 from 14th St. all the way to State Line Interlocking. When operating into the station northbound, the trains would proceed to 12th St. and watch for hand signals from the switchtenders who governed all train movements into the station. Led by F3a 210, THE THOROUGHBRED has just cleared 14th and is beginning to gather speed. Ahead are several curves and the 21st interlocker. *(George Berisso)*

ABOVE • With F3's 82B and 82A in the lead, train #12, THE TIPPECANOE, has just cleared the 21st interlocking south of Dearborn Station on August 10, 1952 and will arrive at the depot in minutes. At this point #12 is passing the Santa Fe coach yards to the left and the IC mainline from Iowa to the right. The Santa Fe mainline from the west joined the C&WI mainline at 21st St. By 1952 THE TIPPECANOE normally had one of the two streamlined RPO's (11 or 12), 2 to 3 coaches, and either a dinette coach or a parlor diner that had been built for THE THOROUGHBRED. Although the Monon has given up on keeping the roof clean and painted it black, the F unit set still retains the classic Indiana University colors, a light gray top, red nose and middle section, and a dark gray bottom. *(Russell F. Munroe)*

The early evening sun shines on F3a 209 as she leads #5 through the 21st interlocking. The engines are crossing over the joint Santa Fe and Illinois Central Iowa division tracks while the express cars are banging across the Pennsylvania mainline. To the left is the GM&O mainline curving off the Chicago River bridge, and to the right is the Santa Fe coach yard. The old Chicago skyline towers in the background. June 1966. *(Matthew Herson)*

Above • Led by F3a 81A, #6, THE THOROUGHBRED, rolls through the interlocking at 74th St. in Hamilton Park on Chicago's South Side on September 8, 1960. Wabash passenger trains from Decatur and St. Louis entered the C&WI on the connection to the right. Monon passenger trains and transfers used the CWI mainline for its whole length from Dearborn Station to State Line Jct. In one mile #6 will slow for a stop at Englewood, the only station Monon passenger trains served in Illinois besides Chicago at Dearborn St. Station. *(Al Holtz)*

Above • After THE THOROUGHBRED lost its meal service cars in 1956 its consist was fairly reliable, with two or three cars handling storage mail and express, an RPO car, and usually two or three coaches. This September day #6 has recently rebuilt coach 41 and 46 seat coach 25. Coach 41 was rebuilt from grille coach 65 in 1956. By 1959 almost all Monon passenger cars were painted in the standard red and gray colors with black roofs. The Monon name was red outlined in white. The circular red Monon herald was displayed in the center of the car below the windows. *(Al Holtz)*

15

Above • Two BL2s lead a caboose westbound on the BRC at 75th St. on the way to Clearing Yard. Monon transfers ran on the Belt Ry. from Pullman Jct. 3.37 west to 80th St., where they crossed the C&WI mainline, continuing another 4.65 miles to Clearing Yard. Normally the train would deliver cars in both directions, so this day's caboose hop is unusual. Chicago, July 31, 1969.
(John Buchanan, Richard Wallin collection)

Above • Southbound Thoroughbred #5 of September 6, 1960 is running short tonight with one baggage, one RPO and two coaches. Monon's management has recently decided that maintaining two separate paint schemes for passenger and freight service is too expensive. So the first coach has recently been repainted in black and gold. Over the next four years most of the remaining passenger cars and all of the F3's will be repainted. Number 5 is on the C&WI mainline at Burnside. The RI branch to South Chicago and the BRC mainline parallel the C&WI from 87th St. through Burnside to Pullman Jct. In just a moment #5 will pass under the Illinois Central mainline and slow for the crossing of the Nickel Plate mainline at Pullman Jct. *(Al Holtz)*

ABOVE • Pullman Jct. was one of the most elaborate junctions in the Chicago area. A northbound train on the C&WI was required to stop short of the junction. It could not proceed until the operator set two tilting target signals, moved a gate, and then gave a proper hand signal. A Monon transfer has just received the hand signal and it is crossing the NKP and RI tracks as it curves westward with a transfer to the BRC led by RS2 53 in May of 1968. *(Robert J. Zelisko)*

ABOVE • Monon F3a 207 leads a southbound transfer at Pullman Jct. on April 7, 1967. The train is leaving the BRC mainline and crossing the Rock Island line to enter the C&WI. The BRC transfer typically had 40 to 70 cars received from many different connecting lines around Chicago. In later years Monon ran direct transfers to the CNW, the Milwaukee Road, and the Soo Line via the C&WI. The Milwaukee Road transfers accessed Galewood Yard by running through Union Station to connect to the MILW main line. *(Richard Wallin)*

RIGHT • The day is cool and crisp; November 6, 1949. Rolling down the C&WI main at 50mph through Burnham Interlocking over the Pennsylvania's Bernice Cutoff, #5 will soon slow to 40mph for the State Line Interlocking. To the right is South Shore's Burnham yard and to the left is the Nickel Plate mainline. State Line Interlocking is one mile ahead. Although the Monon owned the trackage south of State Line, the C&WI dispatcher controlled the movement of trains all the way to South Hammond Yard at milepost 23.2. *(Sanford Goodrick)*

ABOVE • Over the years Monon had as many as six yard jobs assigned to South Hammond that also operated transfers into Chicago. Two yard crews went on duty at the approximate time #70 arrived from Louisville. The yard crew that went on duty at 8:00AM switched #70 from the north end of the yard, assembled the Clearing Transfer, and delivered it to the BRC via the C&WI connection at 80th St. At Clearing the transfer would pick up connecting traffic for #71 and deliver it as quickly as possible to South Hammond. Since the Clearing transfer was usually the largest of the transfers, it was assigned at least two road units. In October of 1969 BL2 36 and its mate roll westward through the junction at State Line. The transfer will run ten miles on the C&WI before turning onto the BRC. The crew will spend most of their day threading through the many interlockers on Chicago's South Side before setting out and picking up their train in BRC's huge Clearing Yard.

(J. David Ingles, Edward Lewnard collection)

MONON

THE FIRST SUB-DIVISION

State Line Tower to Shops Yard

Northern Division		
FIRST SUB-DIVISION		
Chicago	STATIONS	
.....	CHICAGO	N
9.8	19.8	
	State Line	
10.7	.9	
	Hammond	
	2.5	
13.2	South Hammond	N
	2.3	
15.5	Penna. Maynard	
	0.3	
15.8	G. T. Crossing	
	3.2	
19.0	M.C. ⎫ Dyer	N
	E.J.&E. ⎭ 4.5	
23.5	St. John	N
	N.Y.C. 6.0	
29.5	Cedar Lake	
	5.3	
34.8	Lowell	D
	7.8	
42.6	Shelby	N
	N.Y.C. 3.9	
46.5	Rose Lawn	
	11.6	
58.1	Surrey	
	4.9	
63.0	Rensselaer	D
	4.0	
67.0	Pleasant Ridge	
	6.1	
73.1	Lee	
	5.3	
78.4	MONON	N
C.I.&L.		
78.4	MONON	
	7.4	
85.8	Reynolds	
	Penna. 6.3	
92.1	Chalmers	D
	4.1	
96.2	Brookston	D
	4.0	
100.2	Ash Grove	
	7.7	
107.9	SHOPS	N

ABOVE • The Clearing Transfer returned to Hammond in the early afternoon, passing State Line Tower, a small part of which appears behind the nose of C420 511. State Line was operated by the Indiana Harbor Belt, and was staffed by a crew of three operators and levermen. The C&WI mainline began at State Line with the junction of the Wabash, Erie, and Monon mainlines. The C&O of Indiana ended its joint trackage with the Erie and ran west to its own yard at on the BRC at Rockwell St. The B&OCT and Nickel Plate mainlines crossed the C&WI and each other, while all the roads mentioned above crossed over and connected with branch lines of the IHB and the EJE. Got all that?
(Alfred Jones, John Hanacek collection)

ABOVE • C420 501 takes the signal at State Line as it leads a transfer into Chicago. In addition to the Clearing and Chicago Junction transfers, Monon also ran transfers to the Chicago Produce Terminal, 87th Street (BRC), and Canal Street. Monon maintained a team track at Canal Street for shippers who did not have a siding on a railroad. Before the South Hammond freight house was constructed in 1954, a transfer ran to Dearborn Station in the early afternoon to pick cars from Monon's Chicago freight house, which was immediately adjacent to the station. In the late evening, another transfer brought the less than car load cars to the freight house, switched the team track at Canal Street, and made pickups from the BRC on the way back to South Hammond. By June of 1970 when this transfer headed north the business patterns had changed considerably, and it was no longer necessary to perform these tasks on a daily basis. *(Alfred Jones, John Hanacek collection)*

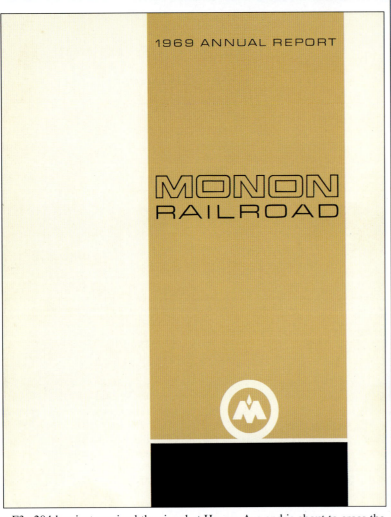

Right • F3a 204 has just received the signal at Homan Ave and is about to cross the Michigan Central and Indiana Harbor Belt lines that ran east/west through Hammond. In about ten minutes the transfer will arrive at South Hammond Yard and the train will be reblocked into #71. If all goes well #71 will leave South Hammond by 9:45PM. *(John Buchanan, Richard Wallin Collection)*

Below • Another Monon transfer that ran north from South Hammond Yard handled the cars for the Chicago Junction and Chicago Stock Yards. When necessary this job also delivered cars to the C&WI at 51st St. In later years the job declined in importance as the traffic to the Stock Yards and the Produce Terminal dried up. On June 11, 1966 H15-44 45 handles a transfer south of State Line. Most of Monon's transfers were of moderate length and tonnage, so a 1500 hp roadswitcher usually proved sufficient for the run to Chicago. *(Russell F. Munroe)*

Right • For many years Monon ran a transfer to the IHB and the B&OCT in the mid-afternoon. Both of the lines crossed the Monon within one mile of the Hammond depot. Monon had a special connection track that allowed it to deliver cuts of cars directly to the IHB near Gibson yard on the east end of Hammond. In turn, the IHB and the B&OCT would usually deliver cars to the Monon during the middle of the day, hopefully in time to make the cutoff for #71 which was due out of South Hammond at 8:00PM. In May of 1966 NW2 13 heads north through downtown Hammond with a transfer cut for the Monon's connections. *(Robert J. Zelisko)*

ABOVE • On March 7, 1959 Richard Baldwin took this picture of Homan Avenue Tower in Hammond from the fireman's seat of #12. Operated by the IHB, the tower governed the movement of trains through the central part of the city. Here the Monon crossed the Indiana Harbor Belt and New York Central (former Michigan Central) mainlines. To the right of the Monon mainline are the Nickel Plate and Erie mainlines. Just beyond the bridge to the north is State Line. A common joke of the time claimed that no thief would be foolish enough to rob a bank in Hammond. He could never get out of the city before the police caught up to him as he would certainly be stopped by a train before he got very far from the bank. *(Richard Baldwin)*

LEFT • Led by F3a 203, #6 crosses the IHB at Homan Ave. in April of 1965. Monon trains ran through this part of Hammond at 25mph. The interlocking threaded a maze of tracks and streets protected by gate operators in the green towers at each intersection. Number 6 is so short that it will not delay anyone very long, but in a few minutes another large freight will surely plod its way through town, much to the dismay and frustration of the motorists of the city.

(Robert J. Zelisko)

RIGHT • THE THOROUGHBRED heads north to Chicago past Homan Ave. on June 28, 1965 with RS2 23 in the lead. A business car trails the lone coach, RPO and baggage car. Number 6 was due into Hammond at 12:20PM and was usually very punctual. The change of engines at South Hammond took about five minutes. Since the South Shore provided a fast, frequent commuter service from Hammond to Chicago, very few passengers boarded the northbound train. Most of Monon's Hammond passengers headed south to the many cities Monon served in the heart of Indiana.

(Robert J. Zelisko)

ABOVE • At 5:29PM BL2 36 led a transfer into Chicago at Homan Ave. As trains were consolidated and enlarged in the late 1960's the schedule of the transfers was modified so that it was not uncommon to catch a train headed to the BRC in the late afternoon. The number of yard jobs was also reduced and the destinations of the transfer changed to meet the shifting situation in Chicago as railroads were merged and interchange points were modified. *(John Buchanan, Richard Wallin collection)*

ABOVE • Monon maintained a joint passenger station with the Erie in Hammond as the two mainlines were adjacent to each other from downtown Hammond to State Line. The Hammond depot was one of the newest on the Monon, having been completed in 1953. When the station was opened it was served by three passenger trains each way, one to Louisville and two to Indianapolis. Erie ran three passenger trains to Jersey City. *(Richard Baldwin)*

ABOVE • Open for public inspection at the Hammond depot, THE HOOSIER sits in the late afternoon sun in all of its glory. The original train set had an RPO baggage with a 30' compartment for sorting the mail, three coaches that seated 46 passengers in comfortable Rotacline chairs, a diner lounge that seated 24 in the dining section and 20 in the bar lounge, and a square ended parlor observation with room for 25 in its "club chairs", 3 in its stateroom, and 11 in its observation room. There were two identical train sets. One set ran south in the morning from Chicago to Indianapolis as #11, THE TIPPECANOE, returning in the afternoon as #14, THE HOOSIER. The other set originated in Indianapolis in the morning as #12, THE TIPPECANOE, ran to Chicago, turned, and became #15, THE HOOSIER. Two more similar train sets arrived later to serve on #5&6, THE THOROUGHBRED, differing in the arrangement of the headend cars and in the fact that they carried a single diner-parlor-observation instead of the separate diner and parlor observation of the Indianapolis trains. F3's 81A&B are polished and bright, but they have already been in service hauling conventional trains while the new streamliners were being finished at Shops. *(Lewis E. Unnewehr)*

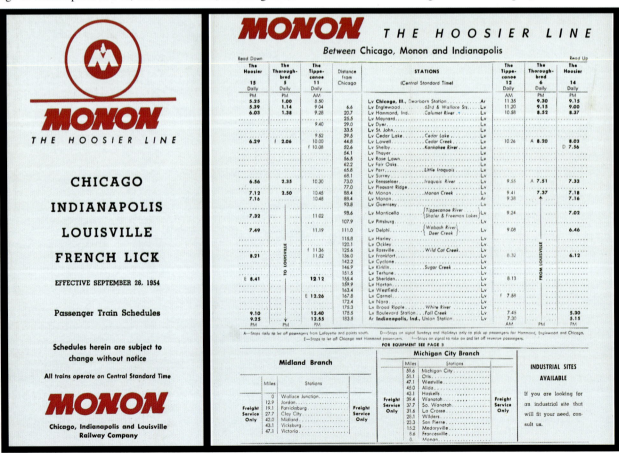

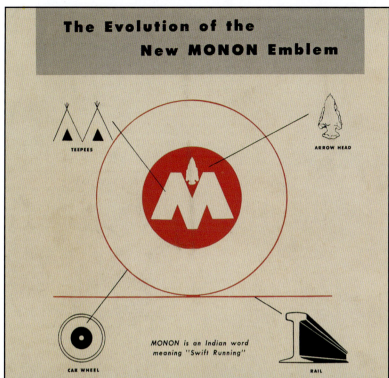

The progressive MONON, The Hoosier Line, enters a second century of service with a new era in Indiana transportation, using Diesel locomotives built by Electro-Motive Division of General Motors.

ABOVE • When the passenger F3's were delivered in May of 1947, they were painted in an attractive arrangement of the red and gray colors of the University of Indiana at Bloomington. White stripes trimmed with gold separated the gray top and bottom of the units from the red center. Note that the gray on the top of the units is a lighter shade than the gray on the pilot and the lower sides. The units proudly display the slanted Monon in speed lettering, the Hoosier Line slogan in fancy script, and a simple version of the new Monon herald just below the cab. The M on the new herald symbolized two teepees joined together, crowned by an arrowhead. Tradition held that the name Monon is was an Indian word that meant swift running, a concept Monon tried to capture with this bright and attractive paint scheme. *(Lewis E. Unnewehr)*

Above • Train #5 pauses at the Hammond station on May 7, 1963, led by RS2 #22. By 1963 most of Monon's passenger cars were repainted black and gold, although the two baggage cars are still in red and gray. Monon's dining and observation cars were retired in 1958, before the transition to black and gold, as were 8 coaches that were retired in 1959 when the Indianapolis trains were discontinued. *(Matthew Herson collection)*

Above • Two F3's led by passenger unit 210 power the southbound transfer from Clearing in the late afternoon in August of 1963. Since Monon was not a wealthy railroad, it could not afford to have its road power sitting all day at an engine terminal between assignments. By the mid sixties it was not uncommon for trains 72 and 73 to be annulled between South Hammond and Shops Yard. Northbound #70 usually arrived at South Hammond about 8:00AM and #71 did not depart until after 8:00PM, so the road power was divided into two smaller power sets and used on transfers into the city. Monon was not fussy about the kind of power that it used, as long as it got the job done. By this date six of the passenger F3's were assigned to freight service, and they were freely intermixed with the 100 series freight F's. *(Roger Puta, Mel Finzer collection)*

Left • Train #5 was due at Hammond at 6:08PM. Note the large number of express and mail cars trailing RS2 23. Monon made a concerted effort in the mid 1960's to get as much head end business for its passenger trains as it could. Normally all of the head end cars ran through to Louisville. Today an L&N baggage car trails the RS2. On most week days there were just enough passengers for one coach. Two or three coaches would be the norm for weekends and college holidays, as Monon served several colleges and universities on the line to Louisville.
(Robert J. Zelisko)

Above • Late in the service era of Monon #5 and #6, THE THOROUGHBRED stops at Hammond while the express section of the RPO is worked by the baggagemen. The C420's were bi-directional units, so it was no longer necessary to take off the road power at South Hammond and add an RS2 to run north to Dearborn Station. The two passenger C420's differed from the freight C420's in that they carried 1600 gallons of fuel and 1500 gallons of water instead of 3100 gallons of fuel in their tanks. Other than the fact that they had a steam generator in their high, short hoods, steam lines, and train air signals, they were identical to the other C420's. The passenger unit modifications cost $30,535 more than the than the price of a basic C420, for a total quoted price to the Monon of $190,695.25 each. *(John Kuehl, Joseph Lewnard collection)*

Left • Shortly after 6PM on September 29, 1967, the last southbound trip of #5 arrives at Hammond. The train is bigger than usual tonight, with two business cars trailing C420 502. Following the baggage car are at least three coaches. The trucks on the engine and the business cars have recently been repainted. The engineer leans out of the cab waiting patiently for the highball from the hind end and in a few moments #5 will resume its seven-hour journey to Louisville. *(John H. Kuehl, Joseph Lewnard collection)*

ABOVE • By May of 1970 C420 502 spent almost all of its service time pulling freights and transfers. Hustling past the Erie Lackawanna yards to the right with the Clearing transfer, it will arrive at South Hammond in five minutes. Monon had a lively interchange with the Erie Lackawanna, but few cars were exchanged at Hammond. Monon preferred to deliver its EL connection cars at Wilders on the Michigan City line, which was about 30 miles southeast of Hammond. There was no need to delay the cars in two different yards, let alone bring them into the congested Chicago switching district.

(Harry L Juday, Edward Lewnard collection)

ABOVE • Hammond was one of the most congested railroad towns in the nation. Railroad tracks crisscrossed the city in every imaginable direction. Given the fact that Monon arrived so early in Hammond it is surprising that Monon served only seven businesses in town. On May 5, 1967 NW2 14 ventured north from South Hammond to switch Monon's most important customer in town, the *Hammond Times*, which received 150-200 cars of newsprint each year. Even after the L&N closed South Hammond yard and diverted the Monon district's freights to Dolton via the GTW at Munster, a local continued to run up the old main line to serve this important customer. *(John H. Kuehl, Joseph Lewnard collection)*

ABOVE • Barely one month before the L&N gained control of the Monon there is a lull in the switching activities and the conductor rests his foot on the footboards of NW2 15 before resuming work. The yard job is standing on the mainline in the late afternoon, helping to set up #71 for its journey south later in the evening. Monon's operations South Hammond were easy to photograph because a city street conveniently ran alongside the west side of the yard from the north to the south end. The middle of the yard was split by very busy 173rd Street, which meant that a train that was ready to start its journey would sit on either side of the crossing until just before its departure. *(James Lewnard)*

ABOVE • The venerable South Hammond roundhouse stood at the southeast end of the yard. At the beginning of dieselization 8 stalls were still in service. Gradually Lafayette Shops took on greater responsibility for the care of the diesel fleet and by the late 1960's almost no significant repairs were done in the roundhouse. Fuel, water and sanding facilities sat immediately north of the turntable to provide for the basic needs of the units visiting the yards.. The turntable was essential for Monon's operations as it was one of the few places north of Monon where the diesels could be turned. There was no wye available at South Hammond for turning cars or trains. In February of 1970, NW2 17 took a spin on the turntable as it was being readied for service on the afternoon switch job. *(Alfred Jones, John Hanacek collection)*

ABOVE ● The servicing facilities at South Hammond were fairly simple, providing fuel, water, and sand to the approximately 15-20 units that visited the yard each day. The large blue water tower in the background belonged to the city of Hammond and was not a part of the railroad's facilities. The two F3's and two BL2's led by F3a 204 are almost completely worn out, but they continue to work on freights and transfers. In 1969 and 1970 Monon frequently assigned four of these older units to #70 and #71 or to the extra freight that ran north of Lafayette approximately four days a week. The railroad was relatively flat north of Lafayette and the four units could more easily handle the 5,000 to 7,000 ton trains on this section without a great risk of a failure out on the road. There were still 5 BL2's and 4 F3a's on the roster in early 1970. Most of them will be set aside when the new U23b's are delivered. March 27, 1970. *(J. David Ingles, Matthew Herson collection)*

ABOVE ● C420 517, U23b 604, and another C420 sit at the South Hammond servicing facility in April of 1970. Freights #70 and #71 typically required a 3 unit, 6,000 hp set of power on the First Subdivision. Occasionally a fourth unit was added. From 1967 until the delivery of the U23b's in 1970, the 18 C420's were the primary road power for the 70 series freights. The remaining F3's and BL2's were usually assigned the Indianapolis (#90-91) and Michigan City (#56-57) freights. The road power did not sit at South Hammond very long, as the units were split apart to power the mid morning transfers to Chicago.

(Alfred Jones, John Hanaceck collection)

ABOVE • RS2 22 lumbers through the South Hammond yard in October of 1966 towing one of Monon's home built extended vision cabooses. Although the RS2's were normally assigned to the locals that ran south of Lafayette, at least one RS2 was kept in Hammond to power #5 & #6 to Dearborn Station. It was thus available to supplement the NW2's on yard assignments from mid evening until noon the next day. The RS2's were also ideally suited to power the local that ran from Lafayette to South Hammond. *(John Hanacek collection)*

ABOVE • In the last month before the L&N merger NW2 15 switches piggybacks from the ramp on the east side of the yard over to the track that #71 is being made up on. Many of these trailers carried Coca-Cola syrup from Chicago to Indianapolis. There were two yard jobs working the afternoon shift on this July day. At the peak of the Barriger era operations Monon assigned 8 yard jobs to switch the six 70 series freights, the two 40 series locals and the transfers into Chicago. Six of these yard jobs also took one of the transfers into Chicago. The crews for these jobs were based at Hammond, while the road crews were based in Lafayette. As traffic patterns shifted and motive power consists were expanded Monon gradually decreased the number of trains operating out of South Hammond. By 1954 trains #74 and #75 were discontinued, and #72 and #73 became extra jobs in the mid 1960's. As the number of freights decreased, so did the number of yard jobs and transfers.

(James E. Lewnard)

ABOVE • In the original Barriger scheme of operations there were six road freights (#70-75) operating between South Hammond and Louisville. Trains #56/57 also ran all the way from Michigan City to Louisville. Since there were five three-unit sets and one two unit set of F3's to power these freights it was imperative that the Monon get the maximum utilization out of the F3's. The road crews normally ran from Shops Yard to South Hammond and turned as quickly as possible on the next train south. On a typical day at South Hammond #70 would arrive about 8AM and its power would turn on #73. Freight 72 arrived in the early evening and its power turned on #75, while #72 arrived about 8:00PM and its power turned on #71. By the time Matt Herson took this photo on July 1, 1966, Monon operated one regular freight (#70 and #71) and one local (three days a week north and three days a week south) between South Hammond and Lafayette each weekday. Since #70 usually arrived in the early morning, the train arriving with C628 404 in the lead must be an extra that was usually called out of Shops Yard about three times a week to handle any extra freight that might need to be moved. From 1964 until 1967 #70-71 and the extras used essentially the same power sets, with two C628's being adequate to handle the trains north of Lafayette.

(Matthew Herson, Edward Lewnard collection)

ABOVE • South Hammond was a long, narrow yard located just slightly east of the Illinois-Indiana border. The yard was divided into two smaller yards. The north yard had 11 tracks and the south yard had 10. Just north of the engine house there was a street crossing protected by a gate operator in a tower. In April of 1970 three brand new U23b's have just arrived with #70, which is standing on the main line. In a moment, the train will pull forward, split the crossing, and the power will cut off. The yard crews will couple on and begin the process of assembling the transfers to Chicago.

(Alfred Jones, John Hanacek collection)

BELOW • Late in the afternoon a transfer powered by U23b's 603 and 601 arrives from the Belt Railway of Chicago's Clearing yard. Monon was a co-owner of the BRC and had the option of delivering its connecting traffic to the BRC at either 87 St. Yard or at Clearing Yard. Since Monon preferred to deliver eastward connecting traffic via interchanges on its Michigan City Line, most of the cars on a transfer were destined for connecting western carriers or local delivery. The Belt served over 380 industrial customer along its lines, all of which were could potentially ship via the Monon with the BRC providing the switching service. Normally a transfer to Clearing would require two road units, with any of Monon's road power being used. Monon also received deliveries directly from into South Hammond Yard from the B&OCT and the IHB, Their transfer units normally ran back to their yards caboose light.

(James Lewnard, Joseph Lewnard collection)

RIGHT • Led by recently rebuilt F3a 82A, #11, THE TIPPECANOE, accelerates from 40mph to 75mph as it passes the south end of South Hammond Yard, on April 27, 1952. The 82a was wrecked on September 17, 1951 when the engineer of #5 inexplicably ran his train around a 15mph curve at the Monon depot at 64mph. The 82A and three other F units derailed, smashing through the stone depot. Both 82a and 81b were rebuilt with F7 style grilles. THE TIPPE-CANOE has typical consist for a morning Indianapolis train: an RPO, two coaches, and a diner-parlor. *(Sanford Goodrick)*

ABOVE • F3a 204 and a BL2 cross the Little Calumet River as they pull the Lafayette local south out of South Hammond Yard in May of 1967. The local normally left South Hammond in the early afternoon on Tuesday, Thursday, and Saturday. The run to Lafayette will take almost eight hours as it will switch all the industrial sidings from South Hammond to Lafayette. The normal power for the local was usually one or two BL2's, which were much easier to switch with than the F3. Climbing up and down the side ladders of these units was not one of the safest activities that a trainman could engage in while performing the necessary moves of placing a car in a siding. In the first years of dieselization a single F unit was used on the local when a BL2 or an RS2 was not available. Since there was another F3 with the same unit number the engine on the local received a temporary number such as 66 or 68. This problem was eliminated when the F3's received the permanent sub-letter A or B in their numberboards. *(Alfred Jones, John Hanacek collection)*

Above ◉ F3's 65b, 65c, and 65a are sitting on the connection track to the GTW at Munster on October 13, 1952. This is an unusual move because most interchange with the GTW was conducted at Haskells on the Michigan City line. The three units wear the latest variation of the black and gold freight colors, which now includes the red Monon herald next to the numberboard and the gold Monon name below the middle porthole. F3b 65c is easily distinguished from the other four B units because it is the only B unit to have a steam generator.

(Sanford Goodrick)

Above ◉ Noted rail photographer Emery Gulash caught two F3a's leading #6 around the sharp curve just south of the interlocker at Dyer, in May of 1965. Just in front of the engines are the diamonds of the EJ&E and Michigan Central lines to Joliet. Monon interchanged 10-12,000 cars with the EJ&E each year, which billed itself as the outer belt line around Chicago. Much of the traffic that Monon received included shipments of steel. A good portion of that steel was waybilled to the Chrysler and Chevrolet auto parts plants in Indianapolis. At least twice a day Monon freights would work the interchange with the J. Most of this traffic never made it to South Hammond. If the cars from the pickups needed to be reblocked, they could be set off at Monon or Lafayette. Dyer was a continuous train order office manned 24 hours a day. The train order board in front of the depot was a common Monon design found in front of many of its train order offices. *(Emery Gulash)*

Above • Monon crossed the New York Central line that ran from Hammond to southern Illinois at St. John, Indiana, 33 miles south of Dearborn Station. Neither railroad interchanged traffic to the other at this location. St. John was a very small community whose grain elevator and lumberyard provided the Monon with only 50 carloads a year. A 56 car siding sat just south of the interlocking. In 1958 #5's departure time from Chicago was changed from 1:00PM to 10AM. Thus #5 was scheduled to meet #12 at St. John. On March 7, 1959 #5 has just cleared the main as #12 approaches and the absolute signal for the NYC interlocker shows a clear. #12 will arrive in Chicago in one hour. *(Richard Baldwin)*

Right • Southbound local #45 sits in the 100 car siding at Shelby with BL2 36 leading, waiting for #12 to pass on March 7, 1959. Just south of the siding Monon crossed the New York Central Kankakee Belt Line that ran from South Bend to Streator and Zearing. The two roads interchanged slightly less than 100 cars here each year. In the early 1950's there were two daily except Sunday locals (#44-45) between South Hammond and Lafayette Shops. They normally took 10 to 12 hours to make their runs as they switched all the industries enroute, with the exception of those located in Monon.
(Richard Baldwin)

Right • One month before the Monon discontinued THE HOOSIER and THE TIPPECANOE to Indianapolis photographer Richard Baldwin received an assignment to accompany a group making a special trip to Chicago. Much to his delight, he was offered a cab ride to Chicago that day. For some reason that he can not recall, #12 made an unscheduled stop in the vicinity of Rose Lawn. While the crew inspected the train he stepped onto the ballast to record #12 for posterity. The expanded consist this March day included two F3a's, a baggage car, an express car, an RPO, and three coaches. *(Richard Baldwin)*

Above ◉ On March 7, 1959 the two TIPPECANOES, #11 and #12, meet. #11 has just cleared the siding switch and the brakeman is walking up to board the last coach. The southbound train has a typical consist for the last month of operation: a baggage car, an RPO, and a coach. *(Richard Baldwin)*

Above ◉ The order board shows a clear signal and the platform is almost deserted at Rensselaer's depot as #12 brakes to a stop. A REA express trucks waits patiently to exchange packages with the express car. Rensselaer, the second largest town on the first subdivision between Hammond and Lafayette, was home to St. Joseph's college, one of many on line schools that Monon proudly served. A typical Indiana farm town, Rensselaer had several grain elevators, implement companies, and fuel stations that provided Monon up to 1200 carloads each year. *(Richard Baldwin)*

RIGHT • Train #6 led by F3a 81A with two baggage cars and two coaches passes the 89 car siding at Pleasant Ridge on May 7, 1961. Monon installed its semaphore signal system on the main line to Indianapolis in 1911. By 1916 semaphore signal were also in service from Monon south to Orleans. From 1924 until 1933 Monon also used an automatic train stop system from Hammond to Monon. Although all of the semaphores north of Monon have been replaced with searchlight signals, many of these semaphores signals remain in service south of Lafayette in 2001! The timetable permitted passenger trains to operate at 75mph over this section of track. *(Don Ball Collection)*

BELOW • Train #12, THE TIPPECANOE takes on passengers at the old stone depot at Monon on April 8, 1950. THE TIPPECANOE has a substitute RPO ahead of its normal consist today. Behind the RPO are two coaches and a diner parlor car. Monon had the shortest route from Chicago to Indianapolis, giving it an advantage over its competitors. Although it was a single-track railroad, it was protected by automatic block signals, which permitted trains to run at 75mph, and there weren't very many freights to get in the way. Monon's route between the two cities was 183 miles, Pennsylvania's route via Logansport was 202 miles, and New York Central's route via Kankakee was 196 miles. *(Sanford Goodrick)*

ABOVE • Budd demonstrator RDC1 sits in front of the old Monon depot on April 8, 1950, waiting to head south to Bloomington. Monon briefly used the Budd car on an experimental service in which the RDC1 made two round trips each day to connect Bloomington and Lafayette with the Indianapolis trains. The depot behind the Budd car won't last much longer than the experiment, as slightly more than one year later (September 17, 1951) a distressed engineer will sail THE THOROUGHBRED around the curve to the left at 64mph. The train's four F3's will demolish the depot. Fortunately, none of the passengers were killed in the accident. *(Sanford Goodrick)*

ABOVE • A modern replacement depot for Monon was constructed as quickly as possible and placed in service in 1953. The depot sat in the center of a complex junction that was the heart of the Monon railroad The photographer is standing on the original Louisville, New Albany, and Chicago mainline that ran from New Albany (and Louisville) to Michigan City. The north south line crossed the former Indianapolis, Delphi, and Chicago right in front of the depot. Curving to the left is the mainline connection that was used by the majority of the trains running north from Lafayette. Another wye track connected the two main lines permitting a train to run from Chicago to Michigan City. There were two yards in Monon, one west of the depot on the Chicago main and one south of the depot on the Louisville main. Both yards could hold 270 cars. Monon had two yard crews, which used an NW2 to switch the yards and the freight house. Almost all of the freights working through Monon had cars to set out and pick up. At Monon trains #70/71 (Chicago to Louisville) and #56/57 (Michigan City to Lafayette) connected to #90/91 which ran as a turn from Indianapolis in the middle of the night. *(Richard Baldwin)*

Above • Train #5 curves off the Chicago main onto the Louisville main in April of 1959. The agent is ready to hoop up the clearance forms and orders and the U.S. Mail is ready to be loaded aboard. The venerable Monon hotel sits just across the tracks from the depot. *(Richard Baldwin)*

Above • The Thoroughbred pulls away from the Monon station and passes the south yard to its right. To the left are the facilities of the Monon Crushed Stone Co., which loaded as many as 1700 carloads a year. Trailing deluxe coach 31, #5 has a typical 1960's consist with an express car, a baggage, and RPO and two coaches. *(Richard Baldwin)*

ABOVE • Photographer Baldwin says that this is a classic small town Indiana picture. The mailbag hangs from the crane for high-speed pickup as THE THOROUGHBRED races past the Brookston depot in April of 1959. Brookston had 1,000 people, a lumber yard, a grain elevator, and three feed companies to generate business for the Monon; though not quite enough business to stop the passenger train. One of Monon's unique crossing devices protects the motorists by proclaiming: "when the light is out, cross at your own risk." The device was supposed to display a green light until a train approached. *(Richard Baldwin)*

ABOVE • By 1964 it was rare to catch red and gray passenger cars in service, as the Lafayette Shops had been working hard to repaint the 27 remaining cars into black and gold. A newly repainted RPO-baggage with silver trucks was added to the rear of #6 at Shops Yard. The train is passing under the U.S. 52 overpass as it heads north past the yard leads in Lafayette. Apparently there was no RPO service on Sundays since the postal cars are frequently absent from trains photographed in this time period and it appears the photographers frequently photographed #5/6 on Sundays! The RPO on today's train is not in its normal position. *(Richard Baldwin)*

MONON

Shops Yard to McDoel Lafayette

The Fourth Sub-division

ABOVE • Freight F3's 63A and 64A sit in front of the Lafayette Shops on August 10, 1958. Lafayette Shops could handle almost any task that was assigned. In 1947 the streamlined passenger car fleet was created out of recently built United States Army hospital cars. In 1956/57 eight wide vision cabooses were built. In 1960 the FM diesels were re-engined with EMD prime movers and in 1965/66 the RS2's were rebuilt. Company records indicate that the freight car fleet was renewed and repainted at Shops every 8 to 10 years. *(Richard Baldwin)*

BELOW • By November 5, 1967, when this picture of F3a 204 and BL2's 32 and 35 was taken, most of the road freight work was handled by the C420's. A three unit set of F's and BL2's typically handled #56 and #57 to Michigan City or took a turn to serve the coal mines on the Midland branch. Only three or four F3's would still be operating by this time. The 100 series F3a's and 300 series F3b's were taken out of service as the more modern Alco centuries were delivered. By 1967 only the former passenger F3's were still in service. *(Don Ball collection)*

Distance from Chicago	SOUTHERN DIVISION Fourth Sub-Division
	STATIONS
117.9	SHOPS 2.1
120.0	Lafayette
	NYC 1.5
121.5	Wab.-Lafayette Jct.
	NYC & St. L. 5.0
126.5	Taylor 6.4
132.9	Romney 4.1
137.0	Linden
	NYC&StL 7.0
144.0	Manchester 3.3
147.3	Crawfordsville 1.1
148.4	NYC Ames
	Penna. 5.5
153.9	Whitesville 3.9
157.8	Ladoga 4.4
162.2	Roachdale
	B. & O. 6.5
168.7	Bainbridge 4.3
173.0	Cary 4.8
177.8	NYC Greencastle 2.2
180.0	Limedale
	Penna. 0.6
180.6	Cement 8.6
189.2	Cloverdale 4.8
194.0	Wallace Jct. 3.8
197.8	Spring Cave 5.3
203.1	Gosport Jct.
	Penna. 0.8
203.9	Gosport 8.3
212.2	Adams 0.9
213.1	Ellettsville 4.8
217.9	Hunters 2.6
220.5	Bloomington
	I.C. 1.0
221.5	McDOEL

Above • BL2 32 sits in between the Shops complex and the yard awaiting servicing in July of 1968. The Shops complex sat above the yard on a level plateau of land connected by tracks on a short grade that descended to connect into the yard at the south end. Monon got its money's worth out of the BL2's, using them in almost any imaginable service including an occasional passenger run. But by this point in time the BL2's were pretty well worn out and many of them have been retired. Although distinctive in design and just as powerful as an F3, the BL2's proved to be awkward when used for switching and prone to cracked frames when used in larger lashups. BL2 32 will be a survivor. The L&N will donate it to the Kentucky Railway Museum shortly after the merger. In later years the 32 will return to the Monon for several excursions and even make a special trip back to its birthplace to help EMD celebrate its big 50th anniversary. *(James Lewnard)*

Above • In August of 1958 a group of fans chartered Monon business car 1 and rode #6 from Louisville to Lafayette. When they arrived there #1 was taken off for servicing and they were given the grand tour of the Shops. Inside the locomotive shop they found NW2 11 and F3a's 83B and 84B being serviced. When the tour was over #1 was placed on the rear of train #5 and the fans returned to Louisville. *(Richard Baldwin)*

ABOVE • RS2 51 sits inside the Shops in April of 1970. Rather than buy new power, Monon completely rebuilt the RS2's in 1965/66. When the Monon dieselized in 1947-49 it favored EMD products over Alco and FM. But in the 1960's the management made a significant change and ordered most of its new power from Alco. Had Alco stayed in the locomotive business it is highly likely that Monon would have become an all-Alco road. The RS2's were durable machines and all of them were still in service when the L&N took over the Monon in 1971.

(William J. Brennan, Robert Yanosey collection)

ABOVE • Passenger F3a 85B is serviced at Lafayette on August 10, 1958. Although they spent most of their service lives painted black and gold, the 85A&B were passenger engines. They were former EMD demonstrators. Together with 62B and 64A they were unique because they did not have the second headlight on the nose door. All trains passing through Lafayette changed crews at Shops Yard. Locomotives were inspected and engine consists were changed out as necessary. Passenger units were changed out at least once a week. Since the railroad was much more rugged south of Lafayette, the motive power consists on most freight trains were expanded with one or two units as the freight trains were re-blocked by the yard crews. (Richard Baldwin)

ABOVE • There was only one FM H10-44 on the Monon, number 18, which spent almost its whole service life in the Lafayette yards. John Barriger had worked for FM before he came to the Monon, and perhaps out of loyalty for his former employer the Monon ordered 3 FM units. Their opposed piston power plants proved troublesome and expensive to repair, and Monon didn't have the time or the money that the Milwaukee or the CNW had to take care of their little fleet. In 1961 the Shops tuned 18 into an oddly shaped NW2, and two years later it was sold to W. R. Grace Chemical Co. Shops Yard was the largest on the system and all of the freights either exchanged blocks of cars or were re-switched here. Five yard crews worked the yard each day, requiring the service of 18 and an NW2. In addition to switching the trains, the yard jobs delivered cars to over 40 industries and interchanged with the Wabash, the Nickel Plate, and the Big Four. *(Richard Baldwin)*

ABOVE • The Monon mainline ran right down the middle of 5th St. in Lafayette, trackage that has only recently removed in a very expensive relocation project. Monon ran as many as 14 trains a day down 5th St., much to the consternation of the people of Lafayette. It was the third largest city in Indiana served by the Monon. In 1902 Monon built a beautiful stone depot just slightly north of downtown. Purdue University was a short distance away on the other side of the Wabash River. The 5th St. depot, taken out of service in 1959, still stands in 2002, being used as a community theater with public meeting rooms. *(Richard Baldwin)*

ABOVE • Climbing out of the Wabash river valley on the south side of Lafayette, #5 will soon been up to track speed at 75mph. THE THOROUGHBRED has just cleared Lafayette Jct. where the Monon crossed the joint Big Four and Nickel Plate mainline. The Wabash mainline, located on the hill behind #5, will pass over the Monon mainline on a bridge ahead. THE THOROUGHBRED left Lafayette at 3:30PM and would take another 5 1/2 hours to reach Louisville. F3a 81B leads #5 and although it resembles an F7a, it is an F3. The unit was extensively rebuilt in 1951 after the spectacular wreck at Monon when the locomotives of #5 smashed through the Monon depot and obliterated it. There were two Monon F3's with F7 grilles. *(Gordon Lloyd)*

ABOVE • Linden was a quiet little Indiana town with about 600 people where Monon maintained an important interchange with the Nickel Plate. The NKP gave Monon a reliable connection to St. Louis and points in Ohio and New York, which provided faster service than the Wabash connection in Lafayette. Southbound # 73 connected with a Nickel Plate train that delivered to the Monon by 9:45AM each day. Northbound #70 maintained the connection with the Nickel Plate freights. Led by F3a 203, #6 makes its station stop in November of 1964. The Nickel Plate interchange is just to the right of engine 203. *(Richard Baldwin)*

ABOVE • Train #73 accelerates away from Linden, having just worked the Nickel Plate interchange. Originating at South Hammond at 1:30AM, #73 handled the overflow traffic that #71 had left behind. It picked up the EJ&E interchange at Dyer and worked at Monon. Reblocked and consolidated with #57 at Lafayette, #73 will also pick up and set out at Bloomington. At Bedford it will pick up the Milwaukee Road interchange traffic. #73 normally handled a block of autoracks received from the GTW at Haskells, which was due at Youngstown yard by 5:30PM. Upon arrival, a K&IT switcher will cut off the autoracks and deliver them to the L&N for a mid-evening departure to Atlanta.
(Richard Baldwin)

ABOVE • As is the case with most railroads, the Monon's depots displayed a great variety of design and construction methods. The Crawfordsville depot sat on the north side of town on a broad curve. The depot stills stands in 2002. Amtrak stops at this location, but uses a small passenger shed instead of the classic brick depot. Crawfordsville is the home of Wabash college, one of the last all male schools in the nation. Monon crossed the Peoria and Eastern and the Pennsylvania's Frankfort to Terre Haute line at Ames, a junction located one mile south of the Crawfordsville depot. *(Richard Baldwin)*

Above • Four C420's and an RS2 pull #72 out of the Greencastle siding in April of 1970. In a moment they will pass under the PC (former Big Four) mainline bridge. Operations on the Fourth Subdivision that stretched 104 miles from Lafayette to Bloomington were much more challenging than those of the First Subdivision. A train operating south of Lafayette could handle only 45% of the tonnage permitted on the section from Monon to Lafayette. Trains operating north out of Bloomington frequently required the assistance of a pusher engine out of town, (usually an NW2 coupled onto the caboose). *(John Fuller)*

Right • Located at milepost 27.7 on the Midland branch, the Clay City tower guarded a junction with a New York Central line that ran from Terre Haute to Evansville. This was the only tower operated by the Monon after WWII. Usually the last road to reach a junction point maintained the interlocking facilities. Since Monon was the oldest railroad to serve the region, it was senior to all the other railroads that crossed it as it wound its way north through the state. The one exception was the Clay City tower. The Midland branch left the mainline at Wallace Jct to serve several coal mines that provided considerable tonnage to the Monon. The mines were served by extras operating either from Lafayette or McDoel Yard in Bloomington. Trains operated two or three days a week as they were needed. *(John Fuller)*

ABOVE • Perhaps the most well know depot on the Monon was the ancient brick depot located at Gosport. Built in 1854, it was unique in that the team track ran through the depot, permitting cars to be unloaded within the main structure. Monon crossed the Pennsylvania's Indianapolis to Vincennes line at Gosport. The photographer is standing on the PRR mainline. For many years the Monon and the Pennsylvania ran a joint passenger service between Indianapolis and French Lick via Gosport. On this particular May 1966 day BL2 34 has been assigned to a work extra. *(Richard Baldwin)*

ABOVE • The EMD BL2 was a unique design that could not be mistaken for any other locomotive. It proved to be one of few dead ends in EMD design history. Fortunately for EMD, it realized its mistake, and the GP7 replaced the BL2 as the standard bearer of EMD's roadswitcher line. Unfortunately, by the time the GP7 was available, Monon had completed its dieselization. When the BL2's wore out, Monon's management made a commitment to acquire Alco roadswitchers. After the delivery of BL2's 36-38, the only EMD products that Monon ordered were two SW1's numbered 5 and 6, which arrived three months after the BL2's were delivered. BL2 34 sits quietly in front of the Gosport depot in April of 1966 waiting out a meet. *(Richard Baldwin)*

MONON

McDoel to Youngstown Yard

The Fifth Sub-division

Distance from Chicago	SOUTHERN DIVISION Fifth Sub-Division STATIONS
221.5	McDOEL
	3.2
E 0.3	Clear Creek
	2.2
E 2.5	Diamond
	7.3
232.8	Harrodsburg
	8.1
240.9	Thornton
	4.0
245.1	Bedford Junction
	0.7
245.8	Bedford
	CMSTP&P 3.4
249.2	Sand Pit
	6.1
255.3	Mitchell
	B.&O. 6.2
261.5	Orleans
	3.6
265.1	Leipsic
	10.2
275.3	Smedley
	6.8
282.1	Salem
	1.9
284.0	Fogg
	6.2
290.2	Farrabee
	3.2
293.4	Pekin
	6.1
299.5	Borden
	16.1
315.6	Vernia
	1.9
317.5	New Albany
	Sou.-B. & O.-Penn.
	1.9
319.4	Youngstown
	4.7
324.1	LOUISVILLE

Above ● The Thoroughbred glides to a stop at Bloomington on March 1, 1964 trailing baggage car 103 and two coaches. Bloomington was largest community on the Monon between Lafayette and New Albany as well as home of Indiana University. In the final years of Monon's independence the passenger deficits had become a growing burden, and there had been a proposal to drop all passenger service south of Bloomington. The resulting train would have connected Chicago with all of the Indiana college towns on the Monon, but it would have done little to eliminate Monon's losses. The final solution was to reschedule #5 & #6 so that the service could be provided with one train set and three crews each day. As a result, the towns from Bloomington to Chicago all had reasonable departure times and the towns south of Bloomington were served in the late at night or early in the morning. As long as the trains served Louisville Monon could supplement the train's revenue with storage mail and express shipments. *(Matthew J. Herson)*

Above ● On April 16, 1966 C628 407 leads RS2 56 and C628 408 on a 70 series freight into Bloomington. Monon found that three C628's were often too much power for a typical freight, while two were not quite enough. So recently rebuilt RS2's often spliced a pair of C628's to provide just the right amount of power. In trade, a C628 was often used on a local, a service that the C628's were not well suited to. Bloomington was in the heart of the southern Indiana limestone district, which the Monon served with over twenty industrial spurs extending from Stinesville at M.P. 207 all the way south to M.P. 248 near Bedford.

(Keith Ardinger, Matt Herson collection)

ABOVE • Few railroads could assemble an engine consist like this. Three F3's and a BL2 are joined to both of Monon's H15-44's. Behind the engines is the McDoel roundhouse, which at first glance closely resembled the South Hammond roundhouse. The McDoel roundhouse remained in service much longer than the South Hammond roundhouse. This roundhouse cared for the McDoel yard engines and provided power for as many as five locals each day. The McDoel yard had three yard switcher assignments, which were normally covered by a single NW2. March 1, 1964 *(Tom Smart, Matthew Hersom collection)*

ABOVE • RS2's 21 and 27 prepare to take a local out of McDoel on November 5, 1960. McDoel was the base of operations for as many as five locals a day. These jobs included the local operating south to Louisville, one or two locals that worked the south stone district, a local that worked the north stone district, the French Lick local, a local to Lafayette, and occasionally a local for the Midland Branch. Since all these locals originated and terminated at McDoel, the road freights had a considerable number of cars to pick up and set out each day. The yard jobs were busy blocking the locals, delivering cars to industries, and readying the pickups for the road freights A stiff grade out of town to the north severely limited the tonnage on a road freight, so almost every day an NW2 or an RS2 would shove #70 or #72 north. More trains operated out of McDoel than operated out of Lafayette. Its yard operations were critical to the smooth movement of trains on the Fourth and Fifth subdivisions. *(Tom Smart, Matthew Herson collection)*

ABOVE • When Monon purchased the F3's, the original plan presumed that four ABA sets, supplemented by two AA sets of F3a's, would be sufficient to handle the three road freights in each direction between South Hammond and Youngstown. The units were not supposed to sit still. They were turned and sent out on another train as quickly as possible, often in less than an hour. In later years, as the trains grew in size and several passenger units became available when the Indianapolis trains were discontinued, four or five unit sets became more common. BL2's and RS2's rarely, if ever, ran with the F units until the early 1960's. By that time the trains were much heavier, and Monon could no longer afford to run its trains with pure locomotive sets. When the F3's were delivered they displayed a fancy script " The Hoosier Line" herald and a decorative three-bar stripe around the lower headlight. But by 1952, when this picture was taken, the scheme was being simplified. Look carefully at the F3b. A plain gold Monon has replaced the script Hoosier Line herald. Soon all the F's units will display the simplified scheme. Near Clear Creek, August 23, 1952. *(M.D. McCarter Collection)*

ABOVE • In the last year of Monon's independent operation #73 rolls over a bridge at Harrodsburg, which was located in the middle of the stone district between Bloomington and Bedford. When C420's 503-506 were first delivered they were used on a wide variety of trains to test their potential, while the C628's continued to be the primary power for the 70 series freights. When it was determined that the C420's were much better suited to Monon's needs, the C628's were returned to Alco and another group of C420's took their place. In the last year of operation the U23b's were delivered, and they were freely mixed with the C420's on all of the trains Monon ran. Note that the train is passing a semaphore signal installed in 1916 Many of these signals still serve CSX on the Monon route south of Lafayette in 2002!

(Lloyd Kimble, Michael Sink collection)

RIGHT • When they were purchased the two H15-44's were numbered 36 and 37 after the first group of BL2's. The pair wandered all over the system in local service, often running together. They frequently served on the south end locals switching the stone district around Bloomington and Bedford, as well as on the French Lick Branch. After re-engining by Lafayette Shops in 1960, they tended to stay on the north end of the system, frequently running on #56/57 and Chicago area transfer runs. Unit 46 switches at Bedford of May 8, 1949.
(Charles Herley, collection of Edward Lewnard)

RIGHT • The Bedford yard crew lines up in front of H15-44 46 on May 8, 1949. There were two yard jobs assigned to Bedford, both of which went on duty in the early morning. One job usually had an SW1, the other a roadswitcher. Bedford had 21 industries that provided traffic to the Monon, the largest being the Indiana Limestone Co. that provided almost 1000 cars each year. In a good year Bedford would generate 1500-2000 carloads. In addition to limestone, there was considerable traffic in steel, sand, and cement. The Milwaukee road interchanged with the Monon at Bedford, providing the Monon with 5,000 to 7,000 carloads a year, most of it destined for Monon's connections in Louisville. It should be of little surprise then that the Milwaukee demanded access to Louisville as a condition of the merger with the L&N.
(Charles Herley, collection of Edward Lewnard)

RIGHT • H15-44 46 rests between assignments on May 8, 1949. Shortly after the H15-44's were delivered, Monon opted to purchase more BL2's. The H15-44's were renumbered from 36-37 to 45-46. It is interesting that the Monon decided to renumber the RS2's from the 20 to the 50 series when they were rebuilt, but the FM's were not renumbered when they were re-engined with EMD power plants in 1960. Note that 46 has the original version of the Monon teepee herald on the cab, as well as the script Hoosier Line slogan on the engine compartment hood.
(Charles Herley, collection of Edward Lewnard)

ABOVE • Local #41, led by RS2's 21 and 27, arrives at Bedford on September 3, 1949. #41 was scheduled to leave McDoel at 9:00AM. It will spend most of the day switching the many industries along the line. Originally #41 and #40 operated daily except Sunday, but in later years the operation will be reduced to three days a week northbound and three days a week southbound. Monon avoided running local trains on Sunday. *(Charles Herley, collection of Edward Lewnard)*

ABOVE • John Barriger was noted for his creative ideas to improve Monon service throughout Indiana. He firmly believed that the Monon could provide innovative, reliable, and profitable passenger service with modern equipment. So Monon tested Budd demonstrator RDC1 for two weeks in April of 1950, running it from Bedford to Monon and return on a double daily schedule. The experimental run connected with Indianapolis trains #11 and #12 as well as #14 and #15 at Monon. Before the Great Depression killed the service, Monon had provided a similar service with trains #130-133 to Lafayette as double daily connections to the Indianapolis trains. Budd RDC1 sits in front of the Bedford depot on April 8, 1950.
(Sanford Goodrick)

ABOVE • Under John Barriger the Monon made a concerted effort to provide excellent passenger service on its two main routes. One year after the streamlined HOOSIER and TIPPECANOE were introduced on the Chicago to Indianapolis run, the Chicago to Louisville DAY EXPRESS was transformed into THE THOROUGHBRED. Heavyweight baggage cars and RPO's were reconditioned and repainted for head end service. New coaches and two diner-parlor-observations were rebuilt from USA hospital cars. Although they resembled the parlor observations (71-72) constructed for the Indianapolis trains, the two diner-parlor-observation cars (58-59) were distinctive in their interior arrangements. A complete, full-service kitchen occupied the front of the cars. They seated 10 in the parlor section and 18 in the dining section. On April 16, 1949 THE THOROUGHBRED rolls into Bedford with a typical consist of 2 F3's, a baggage, an RPO, two coaches and a diner-parlor-observation. *(Charles Harley, Edward Lewnard collection)*

RIGHT • C628 406 leads #72 through Mitchell on August 6, 1965. Although #72 will not pickup or set out at Mitchell, it is an important town for the Monon. The Lehigh Portland Cement Company provided almost 1,000 carloads of traffic each year, and the B&O and Monon interchanged almost 5,000 carloads a year. Monon crossed B&O's Cincinnati to St. Louis line at Mitchell, and the B&O gave the Monon a good amount of lumber and wallboard here, much of which was destined for Indianapolis. It might seem strange today, but Monon received many carloads from south end connections that were destined for Indianapolis. This traffic was hauled north to Monon, and then hauled back south on #91. In a similar way, Monon also hauled a lot of starch and processed grain from Indianapolis to its southern connections.
(Tom Smart, Matthew Herson collection)

BELOW • RS2's 21 and 27 roll the southbound local past the depot at Mitchell on August 6, 1965. Freight #73 will be not far behind. The south local departed McDoel about 9AM, after #6 had passed on its way to Chicago. Since a second local that switched the stone district between Bloomington and Bedford preceded it out of McDoel about 7AM, the south local ran to Bedford before it began its task of switching the many industrial sidings on the way to Vernia. In later years one of the south local's most important jobs was to work the Milwaukee Road interchange at Bedford. At Mitchell it also worked the B&O interchange. Dodging in and out of sidings, the local will be passed by #73 and will meet #72 and #70 before its long journey ends.
(Tom Smart, Matthew Herson collection)

LEFT ● Train #73 rattles across the B&O Cincinnati to St. Louis mainline diamonds at Mitchell on August 6, 1965. A typical #73 would have approximately 80 to 100 cars. Much of its traffic came from Lafayette or connected from #57 earlier in the morning. #73 made more stops than #71 to pick up and set out cars on its way to Louisville. Since Monon ran the whole length of the state of Indiana, almost every railroad that ran from east to west had to cross it in some manner. In more recent times, CSX no longer runs trains directly from Lafayette to Louisville, as the Monon mainline has been severed. Trains leave the Monon at Greencastle, travel west on the former NYC St. Louis line, and then head south on the former C&EI at Terre Haute. Turning east on the B&O's St. Louis line at Vincennes, they regain the Monon tracks at Mitchell.
(Tom Smart, Matthew Herson Collection)

LEFT ● THE THOROUGHBRED, #6, stops at Mitchell on April 15, 1967. Scheduled to arrive at 7:40AM, mail will be loaded and a few passengers will board. Although #6 carries a railway postal car behind the 2200 series express car, clerks no longer sort the mail enroute. The two RPO cars, 13 and 19, were usually used for storage mail after the RPO route was canceled by the Post Office on December 31, 1965. The C420 will easily handle the four car train all the way from Louisville to Chicago as the 300-ton weight of the train is well within its rated capacity of 1600 tons on this district.
(Tom Smart, Matthew Herson collection)

The Orleans depot sits resplendent in the light of the sun with brand new Monon Hoosier Line boxcars in the background. The French Lick Branch diverged from mainline at Orleans The Orleans agency was typical of the agencies on the Fifth Subdivision because it was open only during the daytime instead being open of all three shifts, as was more common on the Fourth Subdivision. The Monon crossed only two other railroads in the 96 miles of the Fifth Subdivision from McDoel to New Albany (the Milwaukee at Bedford and the B&O at Mitchell). In the 104 miles of the Fourth Subdivision from Shops yard to McDoel the Monon crossed or passed under 11 other railroads. Four of the junctions on the Fourth Subdivision were busy enough to require operators 24 hours a day, (the Nickel Plate at Linden, the PRR and the NYC at Ames, the B&O at Roachdale, and the PRR at Limedale). In an age before radio communication between trains and dispatchers was common, the operators at the agencies provided the essential link to keep the trains moving when they deviated from their schedules or operated as extras.
(Lloyd Kimble, Michael Sink collection)

ABOVE • Geographically the Monon was divided into two very distinctively different railroads. North of Bainbridge the railroad was relatively flat, with gentle grades and curves. South of Bainbridge, running through Bloomington and in the area from Bedford to New Albany, the railroad had steep grades and frequent, sharp curves that severely limited the tonnage a locomotive could pull. For example, a 1500hp diesel was rated at 2100 tons pulling north from Lafayette to Monon, and 2800 tons from Monon to South Hammond. On the south end the same 1500 hp unit would be rated at only 1300 tons from Youngstown to Bainbridge, with the exception of a 2600 ton limit from Bedford to McDoel. Locals north of Lafayette frequently required only one BL2 or RS2, while the south end locals usually required two units. On August 5, 1967 RS2's 51 and 59 roll the south local towards Orleans on a section of track that is flat and straight. With a large train, all of the 3,000 HP. will be needed to keep the local moving over the rest of the subdivision. (*Don Ball Collection*)

ABOVE • Scheduled to leave Youngstown Yard in the mid-morning, train 72 was supposed to handle cars for the Milwaukee Road at Bedford as well as cars for Bloomington and Lafayette. It would also handle Chicago, Dyer, and Michigan City cars if its normal blocks were light. At McDoel it picked up cars from the French Lick local and the Bloomington area industries. On most days it ran with 4500 to 6500 tons, usually requiring three C628's or four C420's. Led by C628 404, train 72 rolls through Smedley in October of 1964. The C628's were rated at 2500 tons each between Youngstown and Bedford, so this train could have up to 7500 tons trailing. The C420's were rated at 1600 tons, while the F3's, BL2's, and RS2's were rated at 1350 tons. Given the fact that freight cars were on average smaller and lighter than those of today, #72 could easily have up to 120 cars trailing the units.

(*Don Ball Collection*)

Above • RS2's 28 and 24 sit in front of the Salem depot on October 5, 1963. Normally the local would reach Salem by mid day, so the crew might have walked over to a near-by beanary for lunch. Often #71 or #73 would pass by as the crew waited out the meet. One of Monon's sturdy rider cabooses trails the power. These cars were used to transport less than carload traffic between major terminals. The local would stop at most every station along the line to load and unload small items of freight, even if it had no carload traffic for a town on a particular day. *(Tom Smart, Matthew Herson collection)*

Above • The local has cleared the main line to switch some industries in Salem on September 12, 1964. There are eleven industries in Salem that generate almost 1,200 carloads a year. The Smith Cabinet Co. shipped over 300 carloads of TV cabinets each year, and the O.P. Link Co. added 30 some cars load of wooden handles to the total. Add inbound shipments of feed, coal, and oil to the total, and the local could easily spend two hours a day switching in Salem. *(Tom Smart, Matthew Herson collection)*

ABOVE • Every railroad has a bad day, and this is one of them. It seems that the local crew had a little difficulty spotting some cars on the siding at Salem, as UP 190207 got mixed up as to which track it was supposed to go to. Low and behold, #6 has arrived just in time to help the crew inspect the derailed cars. Fortunately the signal next to the siding was not knocked out of service. A serious looking group of trackside supervisors has already arrived, and no doubt #6 will be on its way with the minimum of delay. *(Lloyd Kimble, Michael Sink collection)*

ABOVE • Three F3a's and an F3b power #72 at Pekin on October 20, 1962. F3a 109 was renumbered from 64A in the same month, as were all the other F units. The 50 and 60 series freight A units were renumbered into the 100's, the 80 series passenger F's became the 200's, and the B units became the 300's. Locomotive 109 was one of two F3a's that was built without the middle porthole, as it was one of the units that was built to replace the F units that were wrecked at Ash Grove in June of 1947. When it was built the area between the between the two portholes had air filters and chicken wire, but these were replaced by plain panels in the late 1950's. *(Tom Smart, Matthew Herson collection)*

ABOVE AND RIGHT • A&B On September 17, 1959 a Monon freight derailed several cars alongside the main at Pekin. Monon kept two derricks built by Bucyrus Erie to clean up derailments and perform other heavy lifts. Derrick 80001 was rated at 100 tons and was assigned to Lafayette, while 80003 was rated at 150 tons and was assigned to Bloomington. The 80003 was constructed in 1929 and was powered a vertical fire tube steam engine. Another crowd of local supervisors has come out to "help" the wrecker crew put things back together as 80003 prepares to lift a refrigerator car back onto the main.
(Lloyd Kimble, Michael Sink collection)

ABOVE • Train #72 races along the main at Pekin with F3a 207 in the lead, followed by 2 BL2's and two more F3a's. By this point in time (January, 1969) the use of the older units on the Fifth Subdivision was rare. A more normal lashup would be four C420's. Usually the F's and BL2's were used on the Michigan City trains or on extras to South Hammond. Occasionally Monon changed motive power consists enroute to better match the available power to a particular consist. The power from #72 normally came south on #71 the night before, so the crew at Shops must have had to make a quick power swap before to keep #71 or #70 moving. *(Tom Smart, Matt Herson collection)*

BELOW • Running northbound, extra 22 north arrives at Pekin on September 3, 1966. There were four businesses to switch in Pekin, which generated 600 to 900 carloads each year. Two RS2's are normally needed on the local, which often had forty or fifty cars by the time it reached McDoel yard. There were so many industries between McDoel and Bedford that it was necessary to run one or two extra locals each day, in addition to the local that ran the whole length of the subdivision. During the 1960's the south end local ran from McDoel to Youngstown on Monday-Wednesday-Friday and returned north on Tuesday-Thursday-Saturday. *(Tom Smart, Matthew Herson collection)*

BELOW • Long hood forward is the order of the day as train #72 with C628 405 passes the northbound local in the siding at Pekin with C628 407. The C628's were bi-directional units and they rarely spent more than two hours at the K&IT Youngstown yard. The engines and crew from #71 would turn on #72, and the engines and crew from #73 would turn on #70. After arrival, the engine crew would return to the north end of Youngstown yard to pick up their train and leave as quickly as possible. By 1966 the locals were run as extras, so it was the responsibility of the local crew to stay out of the way of #5 & #6 as well as the scheduled time freights. The dispatcher could help them with a well timed train order, but other wise they kept one eye on the switch list and the other on the timecard as they worked their way through the day. Pekin July 16, 1966. *(Tom Smart, Matthew Herson collection)*

Above ◉ The south end local rolls northbound with C628 407 leading on July 16, 1966. When the local arrived at Borden it spent approximately an hour switching the Borden Cabinet Co. and the Jacobi Saw Mill. The combined industries shipped about 400 cars a year. Switching industries with a C628 must have been challenging. The C628's had been built for coal service and were ballasted to 198 tons. In contrast, an RS2 weighed in at 119 tons and a C420 weighed 130 tons. The crews must have worried that a big C628 would derail on the light rail of the industrial sidings that the locals served. *(Tom Smart, Matthew Herson Collection)*

Above ◉ A five unit set of F3's rolls around a curve on the Fifth Subdivision on September 23, 1963. Very few photographers took pictures of B units. Monon had five F3b's, numbered 61C-65C. (Actually there were six B units, but the first 64C was wrecked at Ash Grove and was replaced by 2nd 64). They are hard to identify as they had a very small number painted on the lower end of the side near the rear of the unit. None of the units had dynamic brakes and only one, 65C, had a steam generator. When they were built they displayed the Hoosier Line slogan in flowing script centered in the middle of the unit. In later years the slogan was replaced with the traditional Monon name displayed in gold. The last recorded use of the F3b's on the author's trains sheets occurred in late 1965 running on extras between Lafayette and South Hammond. *(Tom Smart, Michael Sink collection)*

Right ◉ A long #72 stretches behind the four F3's that power the morning freight north out of Louisville at Vernia. In the original Barriger era operating plan there were four ABA sets of F3's in the 60 series with a spare B unit (65C), and two AA set of F3's in the 50 series to cover the three freights each way between South Hammond and Youngstown (#70-75), as well #56/57 operating south of Lafayette to Louisville. An F unit set was also the normal power for the coal trains on the Midland branch. Units had to be turned quickly and there was not much of a cushion if a unit was damaged or in need of repairs. Gradually the number of trains was reduced as #56-57 south of Lafayette and #74/ 75 were annulled. Six more F units were added to the pool when the Indianapolis passenger trains were discontinued. By April of 1959 Monon could assemble larger four unit lashups of F3's. Thus F3a 103 (the former 61A) leads two B units and a passenger F3a on the ten hour journey to Lafayette. December 15, 1962. *(Tom Smart Matthew Herson collection)*

Above • In the original operating plan of the late 1940's early 1950's, Monon acquired 9 BL2's, 9 RS2's and 2 H15-44's to power its local freights, a total of 20 engines. The five locals operating north of Lafayette were usually assigned a single unit, while the four southend locals that ran on the mainline usually required 2 units. Adding a local to French Lick with require 2 units, the total number of roadswitchers required for normal operations would total 15 engines. Two more roadswitchers for trains #90-91, and another for #56-57 would bring the total number of units required for daily operation to 18, which would leave two units to run the transfers around Chicago or to be available as spare units in case of a road failure. Obviously, the scheduling of the units was tight, and there was not much room to maintain out of service engines. On August 17, 1960 RS2's 21 and 24 power the south end local at Vernia.
(Tom Smart, Matthew Herson collection)

Above • In April of 1963 a four unit set of F3's lead by 110 splits the semaphores at M.P. 296. The Alco C628's will arrive in 11 months and the F's will soon be displaced to secondary runs. Lead unit 110 was built as 51B, part of a two-unit F3 set constructed in 1946. In 1947 F units sets 62 and 64 were involved in the famous head on collision at Ash Grove. Since Monon was very short of serviceable units, surviving F3a 64B (1st) was renumbered 62B to replace the wrecked unit of the same number and run with survivors 62A and 62C to form a new three unit set. Units 51B was renumbered 64B while its mate 51A was renumbered 64A (2nd) to replace the original 64A which had been destroyed, to form a two unit set, as B unit 64C had also been destroyed. (*Don Ball Collection*)

Right • Train #70 sits in the siding at Vernia waiting to meet #5. The lead unit, 62B, and her sister unit 64A were unique among Monon F units in that they did not have three portholes on their sides. They were purchased along with B unit 64C to replace the original 62B, 64A and 64C that were destroyed in the spectacular head on collision between #75 and #70 at Ash Grove on June 3, 1947. Train #70 left Youngstown yard in the early evening. The train was normally blocked with the NKP Linden cars and GTW Haskells cars on the head end, followed by the EJE Dyer and South Hammond cars. If there was room the train also handled blocks for Bloomington and Lafayette. Chicago cars were picked up at Lafayette and Monon. The operating instructions for the train state "This schedule is very difficult to maintain and #70 cannot be used for other work without seriously affecting the performance".

(*Matthew Herson collection*)

Above • Two C628's hold the main at Vernia with #73 on May 30, 1965. Monon received approximately 450 cars each day from its connections and from the industries along the line. Each one of the road freights would carry approximately 60-75 of those loads each day. A good portion of the cars Monon received was bridge traffic between two other railroads. It was common, for example, for #72 to leave Youngstown yard with a block of cars for the Nickel Plate at Linden, destined for St. Louis or points in the east. In a similar move, Wabash would deliver auto parts to Monon at Lafayette Jct. for forwarding to the Ford plant in Louisville that would be placed on the head end of #71 for delivery at 7:15AM. *(Tom Smart, Matthew Herson collection)*

Above • C420 517 assists three sister C420's on #71 at Vernia on June 29, 1968. They will arrive at the K&IT Youngstown yard in about 30 minutes. Train #71 was Monon's principal train on the Louisville line. All other freights were required to clear its schedule. #71 was due in Louisville in the early morning (5-7AM) It had hot connections to Southern and L&N freights as well as the L&N transfer to the Ford plant. The train was assembled at South Hammond with the majority of its cars coming from the BRC and the Chicago Junction. It carried a block for Indianapolis to set off at Monon for #91, as well as blocks for Lafayette, Bloomington, New Albany and Louisville. At Monon it picked up carloads of TV cabinets from Monticello for RCA in Bloomington. At Lafayette the Wabash set off a block of auto parts by 11:00PM that was picked up immediately by a yard engine to be set into the Louisville block.

(Tom Smart, Matthew Herson collection)

ABOVE • Racing through Vernia in the early evening of July 8 1962, #5 has one more stop before it arrives in Louisville. Two coaches were more than sufficient to carry the passengers south of Bloomington. On weekends a third or fourth coach might be added. College holidays would stretch the equipment, but cars could be added at Lafayette or Bloomington as they were needed. By 1962 Monon kept seven coaches for the two sets of equipment need to run THE THOROUGHBRED.
(Tom Smart, Matthew Herson collection)

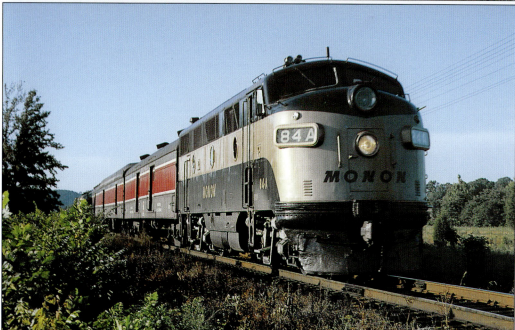

LEFT • THE THOROUGHBRED passes by Hausfeldt Lane on July 12, 1962, its journey to Louisville will soon be at an end. Engine 84A has spent most of its career working in passenger service. It will soon be renumbered 207 and continue in passenger service until the arrival of C420's 501 and 502 in 1966.
(Tom Smart, Matthew Herson collection)

BELOW • With a train as short as #5 it is little wonder that Monon made several attempts to discontinue its passenger service to Louisville. F3a 202 leads #5 into New Albany on April 20, 1962. Two sets of equipment were still being used to provide daylight passenger service from Louisville to Chicago. In 1964 the schedule will be altered so that one set of equipment was needed for the daily round trip. Monon will also solicit more express business in an effort to make the train pay for itself. Crews for #5 & #6 were based in Lafayette. At 7:30PM a crew would go on duty at Lafayette for #5, taking it south to Louisville. The train arrived at 1:10AM and the crew rested until 5:00AM. The same crew then took #6 north to Lafayette, arriving at 10:30AM. Another crew then boarded #6, taking it north to Chicago. They laid over at Dearborn station from 1:30PM until 5:00PM, at which time they brought #5 back to Lafayette, completing the cycle. *(Tom Smart, Matthew Herson collection)*

ABOVE • After the Indianapolis passenger trains were discontinued, Monon only needed four F units to cover #5 & #6. The other six passenger F3's were rotated in and out of freight service as needed. There was one passenger F3b 65C, which had been built as an EMD demonstrator and was equipped with a steam generator. In the renumbering of 1961 65C became 305. Always painted in black and gold, 65C was used occasionally on large passenger trains but was rarely needed in passenger service in the 1960's. On October 5, 1963 passenger F3a 210 leads two F3b's and another F3a on a 70 series freight at New Albany. *(Tom Smart Matthew Herson collection)*

LEFT • The evening sun is setting as #5 arrives at New Albany in June of 1962. Surprisingly, all of the passenger cars following F3a 84B are still painted red and gray. Tonight the train has an express car rebuilt from a troop kitchen, two baggage cars, an RPO, and a coach. The train was given forty minutes to run the 6.6 miles to Louisville's Union Station. At New Albany the Monon trains left home rails, running on the Kentucky and Indiana Terminal across the Ohio River to either Youngstown Yard or Union Station. The L&N switched the train and serviced the passenger cars at Union Station.
(Tom Smart, Matthew Herson collection)

Monon served 25 industries in New Albany that produced over 3000 carloads a year. To serve these industries and work the Southern interchange a switch crew went on duty at 6:30AM at Youngstown Yard. They worked all day in New Albany, setting up as many cars as possible for local #40 to take north in the mid morning. After they completed their work, they took the remaining cars back across the Ohio River to the K&IT. One of Monon's two SW1's was often assigned to this job, but today it is in the care of NW2 15. This was Monon's only regular switch job assigned to the Louisville area. *(Matthew Herson collection)*

ABOVE • The track layout at New Albany revealed how old the Monon really was. In the early years of railroad construction it was common to build the mainline right down a street. Monon had four locations where trains and automobiles had to share the right of way. Needless to say in the 1960's the street trackage presented an operational headache and the railroad would much have preferred to reroute its mainline around these towns. But rerouting the street trackage in New Albany would have cost the railroad far more money than it would ever have available (The rerouting of the tracks in Lafayette in 2001 cost $180 million). So C628 leads train #73 slowly down the street on June 30, 1965, as another generation of trains will continue to do until present day.
(Tom Smart, Matthew Herson collection)

ABOVE • Train #71 has a special delivery to make on October 2, 1965 in the form of a brand new Southern SD35. The EMD plant in McCook was located on the joint IHB-B&OCT mainline. Both belt lines delivered to the Monon at South Hammond. The journey for new units via the Monon was fairly swift. If the belt lines could deliver the new units to the Monon by late afternoon, they would be on their way to Louisville by late evening and delivered to the K&IT by noon the next day. *(Tom Smart, Matthew Herson Collection)*

ABOVE • Local #41 arrives at Vincennes St. in New Albany on May 13, 1950. H15-44's 45 and 46 are in the lead as the train prepares to cross the K&IT Ohio River bridge. Immediately behind the locomotives is one of nine former Army kitchen cars that were rebuilt into rider cabooses numbered C213 to C221. Apparently these cars were not well suited to the task, as they were replaced by 1956 with four homebuilt rider cabooses constructed on gondola frames. Company records indicate that several of the troop kitchen rider cabooses were converted into express cars. *(Charles Herley, collection of Edward Lewnard)*

ABOVE • C628's 408, 402, and 400 pull #70 off of the Ohio River Bridge on March 26, 1967. The crews for the Fifth Subdivision freights were based at McDoel Yard in Bloomington. Typically a crew would run south on #73 and return immediately on #70, or run south on #71 and turn on #72. Three C628's were the normal power for a 70 series freight from 1964 until 1967. A three-unit set could handle 6600 ton from Youngstown to Bedford and 13200 tons from Bedford to McDoel. Southbound they were rated at 6600 tons for the whole trip.

(Tom Smart, Matthew Herson collection)

ABOVE • A Monon freight led by C628 402 passes a Southern freight led by SD35 3009 as they both descend from the K&IT Ohio River bridge on May 6, 1967. The 4,039 feet long bridge had a toll highway on either side of its double track mainline. Trains from joint owners B&O, Monon, and Southern used the bridge to access Louisville. The bridge was built in 1912, replacing an older structure built in 1885. *(J. David Ingles, collection of Edward Lewnard)*

ABOVE • Monon freights entered Youngstown Yard as they descended the grade from the K&IT Ohio River bridge. There was a double wye at the foot of the bridge that allowed trains to proceed south to Youngstown yard or to head east to a connection with the Illinois Central and Pennsylvania tracks near the Louisville Bridge that was used by the Pennsylvania to cross the Ohio River. The K&IT mainline was double tracked all the way from the K&IT Bridge to the L&N connection just south of Union Station. Monon C628 leads two more C628's as they round the curve coming off the K&IT Bridge on July 4, 1964. *(Matthew Herson collection)*

Train #70 leaves Youngstown Yard on June 12, 1965 behind C628's 402 and 401. The K&IT performed all of the switching for the owner lines, made interchange deliveries to the non-owner lines, and handled cars to more than 225 industries in the Louisville area. In a normal year the K&IT would handle over 775,000 cars through its facilities. Interchange between the owner lines took place within the confines of Youngstown Yard. The K&IT also provided its owners with complete servicing facilities for locomotives and freight cars. A large roundhouse and servicing facility stood in the northwest section of the yard. *(Tom Smart, Matthew Herson collection)*

ABOVE • In late June of 1962 a four unit set of F3's lead by 63B pulls #72 toward the K&IT bridge as it leaves Youngstown Yard. Deliveries from the connecting roads were made around the clock in Youngstown Yard. Cars for #70 had to be ready by 5:15PM and for #72 by 9:15AM. Louisville was the heaviest interchange point for the Monon, with L&N providing twice as much business as the Southern. *(Tom Smart, Matthew Herson collection)*

Left • Five RS2's, 24, 21, 25, 27, and 28 sit under the massive coaling tower at Youngstown on March 3, 1963. Most of these units will be needed the next morning to power the four locals that worked out of McDoel Yard in Bloomington. Since there were fewer locals operating on Saturday or Sunday, Monon would gather the units together and run them on a road freight to Youngstown. Thus, the F units on a road freight could be turned at Bloomington while the RS2's handled a round trip to Louisville. When coal traffic from the Southern connection at French Lick was heavy Monon frequently ran a 2nd # 72 between Bloomington and Lafayette, especially on a Saturday night. This practice brought the local power to Shops for inspection and rotation. On Sunday the power was returned to McDoel Yard, ready for the next trip on Monday morning.

(Tom Smart, Matthew Herson collection)

ABOVE • In the early 60's Monon followed the example of many railroads by running fewer, longer, and heavier freights. As labor costs rose in the 1960's, there was a lot of pressure to run bigger, more efficient trains while reducing the number of crews and trains. Three or four F units were often insufficient for the larger trains on the Fifth sub-division. On February 23, 1964 Monon ran a we aren't mad at anybody lashup, with a BL2, an ABA F3 set, an H15-44, and an RS2. In all likelihood, the last two units will probably be taken off at McDoel yard to power one of the locals on the next day. *(Tom Smart, Matthew Herson collection)*

BELOW • Since Monon used the K&IT Youngstown yard in Louisville to conduct its business, it had no engine facilities of its own at the southern end of its system. Here F3a 104 rides the turntable at Youngstown in October of 1963. On any given day the power of the Southern, B&O, K&IT, and Monon was freely intermixed at the servicing facilities. The 100 class F3a's and 300 class F3b's still rule the main line, but the C628's will be delivered in six months. F3a 104 was built as 61A in 1946, was renumbered 104 in 1961, and ran until 1966 when it was traded in on a C420. *(Tom Smart, Matthew Herson collection)*

RIGHT • Three months after the Monon discontinued regular passenger service C420 502 sits at Louisville with a coach and business car for a director's special, ready to head back north. Monon continued to run Derby Specials and football specials into 1971. One of the last Monon passenger trains to run was a Derby Special in May of 1971 that had to use Illinois Central Station in Chicago, as Dearborn Station closed on May 2nd, the last day Santa Fe operated a passenger train into Chicago. Amtrak had taken over regular passenger service on May 1st, and Monon merged with the L&N on July 31st. *(Tom Smart, Matthew Herson collection)*

MONON

The Indianapolis Line
Monon to Indianapolis

THE SECOND SUB-DIVISION

ABOVE • THE TIPPECANOE, #11, rumbles across the Wildcat Creek trestle north of Rossville in March of 1959. Trailing F3a 82A are an RPO, a baggage, and two coaches. The train was restricted to 25mph on this bridge. Monon's two longest bridges were located on the 2nd Subdivision. The Wabash River bridge at Delphi was 1212 feet long, and the Wildcat bridge was 1278 feet long. *(Richard Baldwin)*

ABOVE • Ten miles south of Monon on the Indianapolis line, Monticello appears to be a sleepy Indiana village as #12 prepares to stop on March 7, 1959. Monticello was the location of a large RCA factory that made wooden TV cabinets for the RCA plant in Bloomington. After locals #46/47 were dropped in the early 1960's, Monon ran a local south from Monon to Monticello every weekday, usually powered by a BL2. In addition to its switching duties in Monticello, the local would also run south to the small village of Harley. Along the way it worked the industries and the Wabash interchange at Delphi. After completing its work, the local returned to Monon, rearranged its cars, and then proceeded north to Wanatah on the Michigan City line. When it completed its work, the local returned to Monon a second time, ready to deliver its cars to #71 in the late evening. *(Richard Baldwin)*

NORTHERN DIVISION
SECOND SUB-DIVISION

Distance from Chicago		STATIONS	
88.4	C.I.&L.	MONON	N
		5.4	
93.8		Guernsey	
		4.8	
98.6	Penna.	Monticello	D
		9.3	
107.9		Pittsburg	
		2.5	
110.4		North Delphi	
		0.6	
111.0	Wabash	Delphi	D
		4.8	
115.8		Harley	
		9.8	
125.6		Rossville	D
		10.4	
136.0	N.Y.C.&St.L. Penna.	Frankfort	D
		10.9	
146.9		Kirklin	D
		8.5	
155.4		Sheridan	D
		8.0	
163.4	C.I.	Westfield	D
		4.4	
167.8		Carmel	D
		4.6	
172.4		Nora	
		5.7	
178.1		Fair Grounds	
		0.4	
178.5		Boulevard (38th St.)	
		1.9	
180.4		Belt Junction	D
		1.3	
181.7		Mass. Avenue	
		1.8	
183.5		INDIANAPOLIS	N

RIGHT • Extra 607 south heads through Rossville on its way to Indianapolis in November of 1971. For many years the crews for #90 & #91 were based in Indianapolis, running north to Monon at 10:00PM and returning early the next morning after exchanging cars with #57 and #71. Just before the merger with the L&N this procedure changed. The crews were now called at Monon at 8:00AM, picked up their train in the yard, ran south to Indianapolis, and then returned to Monon. The power from #90/91 no longer laid over at Indianapolis all day, and in theory could be used for other purposes on trains operating out of Monon in the evening. *(Don Ball Collection)*

BELOW • Rossville was a small agricultural town located at MP 125.6 on the Second Subdivision. Typical of many of the communities that the Monon served, it had a grain elevator and a chicken hatchery. Together they generated about 125 carloads a year. Rossville also had a train order office, and was the scheduled meeting point for local #46 and #47. *(William B. Stewart, John Fuller collection)*

Left • The Tippecanoe approaches the Frankfort depot on March 7, 1959. After a short stop it will proceed to a junction with the Pennsylvania Logansport to Terre Haute line as well as the Nickel Plate Ohio to St. Louis mainline. Frankfort generated considerable tonnage for the Monon, with up to 900 carloads a year. Monon's two biggest customers were the California Packing company, which produced canned goods, and Swift & Co., which produced soybean meal and soy oil.

(Richard Baldwin)

ABOVE • Racing under the U.S. 31 bridge north of Indianapolis, #11 hurries to its scheduled 12:10PM arrival at Union Station. Monon maintained the fast four hour, fifteen minute schedule between Chicago and Indianapolis for years. Once diesels were introduced, THE HOOSIER was carded at a flat four hours, and in the last year of service #15 was allowed three hours and fifty minutes to make the run. When this picture was taken in March of 1959, the area surrounding the train was decidedly rural. There weren't very many large towns between Monon and Indianapolis. Number 11 was scheduled to make four regular and two flag stops, while #15 made only four regular stops. *(Richard Baldwin)*

ABOVE • Even in the 1950's Monon was a high-speed railway. Although the cab signals are no longer in service, the semaphore signals still protect the main, and passenger trains are allowed 75mph until they reach the city limits of Indianapolis, where 30mph is required. Approaching Indianapolis from the north, #11 flies across a highway bridge proudly advertising the Hoosier Line. The railway postal and express contracts kept the passenger service alive far longer than the railroad would have been able to sustain the service with passenger receipts, and the train will be in service for slightly less than a month. *(Richard Baldwin)*

BASEBALL SPECIAL

CENTRAL INDIANA RAILWAY CO.
MONON ROUTE

SUNDAY, JULY 20, 1952

LEFT • A troop extra heads north from Indianapolis on an early spring morning in 1958, heading to a connection with another railroad at 51st on the C&WI in Chicago. Monon frequently ran extra trains, including Metropolitan Opera Specials, KofC Specials, Derby trains and footballs trains between the online universities. The six daily passenger trains normally required four two unit sets of F3's (81A&B-84A&B), so 85A&B spent a lot of time running on the extra passenger trains. They also took turns running on the regular schedules, providing maintenance time for the regular units. *(Richard Baldwin)*

ABOVE • Train #14, THE HOOSIER, left Union Station at 4:30PM. Within ten minutes it was running alongside the Indiana State Fairgrounds on the north side of Indianapolis. THE HOOSIER frequently had more express cars than THE TIPPECANOE, and often had two or three coaches. The black and gold passenger units, 85 A and 85B, were considered dual service units, although they spent a considerable amount of time in passenger service. For many years they stayed together as a set, frequently running on freights 70-75 north of Lafayette when a third unit was not required to meet the schedule. *(Richard Baldwin)*

Above • Boulevard Station on the north side of Indianapolis was the first stop for the passenger trains headed to Chicago. Located in the more fashionable section of the city, a considerable number of passengers boarded here rather than make the trip into the central city. In the years before WWII, Monon ran three passenger trains each way between Chicago and Indianapolis. Until 1938, trains #35 and #36, THE MIDNIGHT SPECIALS, ran to Cincinnati via the B&O. THE MIDNIGHT SPECIAL carried Pullmans for Cincinnati, Indianapolis, and for Boulevard. The Pullman for Boulevard was placed on a side track that can be seen behind the main line, running in back of the parked cars. Since #36 left Indianapolis at a the very unrespectable hour of 1:30AM, the patrons of the car were welcome to board at anytime after 9PM. During WWII train service was reduced to one daytime train. When John Barriger modernized the trains in 1947, the service returned to two daily trains, but the overnight service was not restored.

(Richard Baldwin)

Above • F3a 82A arrived at Union Station on #11 at 1:05PM and was scheduled to return to Chicago on #14 at 5:15PM. In between runs it was backed down to the Monon roundhouse at 28th St. on the near north side of Indianapolis. The large brick roundhouse still handled the normal daily servicing of the units assigned to the 2nd subdivision The five active stalls were served by a 78' turntable. The hostlers are fueling the F3, and will turn it on the turntable before returning the unit to Union Station later in the afternoon. *(Richard Baldwin)*

ABOVE • Train #91 normally arrived at Belt Jct. Yard in Indianapolis the early morning. The power was serviced and turned and was available for use on local #46 or in the yard if it was needed. The road freight normally required two 1500 hp units, while locals #46/47 normally required one unit. To efficiently use the power from #91, it was possible for a unit arriving on #91 to turn back on #46. This unit could then be used at Monon during the evening and be turned back south on #47 the next day. Southbound #47's engine would arrive in the early afternoon, and could easily be turned and serviced for #90's departure at 10:00PM. F3a 101 was originally built as 51A in 1947. It was briefly numbered 64A when the original unit of that number was destroyed in the Ash Grove wreck, and them returned to 51A. In the general renumbering it became 101, and remained in service until 1966. Belt Jct. October, 1965. *(Richard Baldwin)*

ABOVE • By 1965 Monon had hired a local fuel company to service the units as they laid over between runs. Locals #46 /47 no longer ran all the way to Indianapolis, so the road power sat the whole day at the roundhouse if not needed for the yard job. For many years the road freights on the Indianapolis line ran at night, switching the industries south of Delphi as they returned to Indianapolis. Monon's principal connection in Indianapolis was the B&O, which received and delivered approximately 3200 carloads a year. Pennsylvania and the NYC also interchanged over 2,000 carloads a year. Interchange with the Illinois Central and the Nickel Plate was less than 300 carloads a year. All deliveries of interchange were done via the Indianapolis Union Ry.

(Richard Baldwin)

Above ● There were three yard jobs assigned to Belt Jct. Yard. Normally an NW2 was the assigned unit, but on this October day in 1965 BL2 37 has the assignment. The first yard job switched #91, worked the north end industries, and switched and turned #11 at Union Station. The second job handled #14 and #15's equipment, switched #47 and made up #90 and the transfer to the Indianapolis Union. The third job turned #15, switched the transfer, made up #46, and switched local industries as needed. Monon had 28 regular customers in Indianapolis, which included 8 lumberyards. The most important customer was Indianapolis Newspapers, which received over 1500 carloads of newsprint a year. Chrysler also received as many as 20 carloads of sand each day which Monon received from the C&O at Michigan City for delivery in Indianapolis. *(Richard Baldwin)*

Above ● Massachusetts Avenue was the southern end of the Monon in Indianapolis. Monon passenger trains to Union Station entered the parallel NKP/Big Four mainlines at this point., The tracks curving off to the right are the main tracks of the Big Four that head east to Ohio. F3a 82B heads train #11, one of the last F units to retain the light gray paint on the top of the unit. By the time this picture was taken in 1957 the F units were painted with dark gray on the top and bottom of the units. *(Richard Baldwin)*

Right ● Train #12, THE TIPPECANOE, passes the block tower at Massachusetts Avenue on March 7, 1959. The turnout is lined for the Monon main. The diverging route connects to the Nickel Plate line that ran north to Michigan City, which the Monon followed for just over a mile north to Belt Jct. Yard. The Nickel Plate yard was adjacent to the Monon yard. The Big Four mainline diverges to the right. In years past a large passenger station stood at this location, (also known as 10th St.). *(Richard Baldwin)*

ABOVE AND BELOW • Train #11, THE TIPPECANOE, passes Ohio St. in March of 1959. At this point the train entered the tracks owed by the Indianapolis Union Ry. It will arrive at Union Station in about five minutes. Number 11 has a typical consist for the last month of passenger operation to Indianapolis: a baggage car, a 30' RPO baggage, and 46-seat coach number 24. The trip from Chicago took four hours and ten minutes. The train will lay over at Belt Jct. yard for about three hours, and return north at 4:30PM. *(Richard Baldwin)*

LEFT • Monon was required to switch its own passenger trains at Indianapolis Union Station since the IU did not supply a switch engine for the use of its tenants. After the observation cars were removed in 1957 it became a common practice to back the train with the road engine from the depot to Belt Jct. to turn and service the train. When necessary, a yard engine would follow the train into the depot, switch the train, set the express and mail cars over to the unloading tracks, and take the remaining cars to Belt Jct. for servicing. In May of 1959 NW2 17 passes Union tower at the east end of the depot with two coaches as it prepares to assemble #14 for its northbound trip to Chicago. *(Richard Baldwin)*

ABOVE • The early morning sun illuminates F3a 82A as it prepares to lead #12 north from Indianapolis Union Station in the spring of 1959. Monon was a tenant of the Union Station, which was operated by the Indianapolis Union Railway. Monon's annual rent equaled 7% of the value of the property plus a similar proportion of the operating and maintenance expenses of the terminal. Unfortunately, the Monon was required to still pay these rents and fees after it discontinued regular passenger service in April of 1959. *(Richard Baldwin)*

ABOVE • Two years after Monon discontinued regular passenger service to Indianapolis a rerouted THOROUGHBRED heads west out of Indianapolis Union Station in August of 1961. Apparently there has been a derailment somewhere south of Bloomington, as #6 came north on the Pennsylvania from Louisville, turned west at Union Tower, and headed through the station. The train is being pulled by a single F3 and is positioned in reverse of its normal running order, with express car 2205 prominently displaying markers on the rear. A good guess would suggest that the train will use the Peoria and Eastern to Ames or the Pennsylvania to Limedale before turning north on the mainline.

(Richard Baldwin)

MONON

The Michigan City Line
Michigan City to Monon and the French Lick Branch

The Third Sub-division

ABOVE • When the Monon was originally constructed by the New Albany and Salem, the directors decided that Michigan City would be the northern terminus of the railroad, connecting the Ohio River with Lake Michigan. In a complicated deal that allowed the Michigan Central to use the New Albany's authority to construct a railroad in Indiana, the MC extended its mainline west from Michigan City to Chicago. In return, the New Albany received trackage rights to Chicago on the MC line and a valuable interchange partner. Over the years the Pere Marquette (C&O) and the South Shore also provided the Monon with interchange traffic. BL2 34 sits in front of the Michigan City freight house in November of 1960, waiting for its next assignment. It displays the original Monon paint scheme for a BL2, with white Monon lettering, a small script Hoosier Line slogan, and the simple version of the Monon herald under the cab window. *(Emery Gulash)*

NORTHERN DIVISION
MICHIGAN CITY BRANCH
THIRD SUB-DIVISION

Monon		STATIONS	
	NYC&StL C.S.S.&S.B. M.C.	MICHIGAN CITY	
.6		1.9	
.7	P.M.	Round House	D
		6.6	
.1	N.Y.C.	Otis	D
		4.0	
.1	Wabash	Westville	
		2.1	
.0	B.&O.	Alida	
		1.9	
.1	G.T.	Haskells	D
		3.7	
.4	Penna.	Wanatah	D
		1.7	
.7	N.Y.C.&St.L.	South Wanatah	N
		5.2	
.5	C.&O.	C. & O. Crossing	N
		0.9	
.6	Penna.	LaCrosse	
		3.5	
.1	Erie	Wilders	
		4.8	
.3	N.Y.C.	San Pierre	D
		8.1	
.2		Medaryville	D
		6.6	
.6		Francesville	D
		8.6	
	C.I.&L.	MONON	N

ABOVE • When Emery Gulash took this picture of the Michigan City freight house in 1963 it was over 100 years old. A sturdy building of solid brick, it had a large door in the front that permitted freight cars to be placed inside for loading and unloading merchandise. The last scheduled passenger trains on the Michigan City Line were #9 and #14, which were discontinued in 1928. *(Emery Gulash)*

ABOVE • The Michigan City yard crew went on duty at 7:45AM, shortly after the arrival of #56 from Lafayette. Normally the crew used one of the roadswitchers from #56 for its power. Monon served twelve customers in Michigan City, which shipped or received about 1400 carloads a year. Pullman-Standard was Monon's most important customer. The new freight cars shipped from Pullman-Standard's shop accounted for 80% of Monon's local business. A good portion of this business was exchanged with the Erie (EL) at Wilders, located 21 miles south of Michigan City. In April of 1963 BL2 34 pulls the yard job past the Pullman-Standard switch engine 5, which is delivering a cut of new Santa Fe damage free plug door box cars from the plant.

(Emery Gulash)

ABOVE • The majority of Monon's business at Michigan City was the interchange with the three connecting railroads. Monon and the South Shore exchanged over 10,000 carloads a year, while the C&O and the NYC (MC) both provided about 4,000 carloads a year. A considerable percentage of these loads included coal for the steel mills around Chicago and foundry sand and newsprint headed to Indianapolis. A South Shore freight clears the diamond as BL2 34 pulls up to the junction in April of 1963.

(Emery Gulash)

ABOVE • For many years road freights #56 and #57 required only one 1500HP unit, which was usually a BL2. In the 1960's the train often grew to 70 cars and 4,000 tons, so a second unit was needed. F3a 109 sits in front of the Michigan City freight house waiting for its companion to finish switching the yard. In the early evening the two units will be rejoined and #57 will head south at about 9:45PM. By the 1960's it was a common practice to leave an engine overnight at Michigan City as #56 frequently arrived late. At times an F3a would be used on the yard job, although a roadswitcher was certainly preferred over the F unit. *(Owen Leander, collection of Edward Lewnard)*

ABOVE • On September 24, 1964 #56 arrived at Michigan City with a BL2 and two F3a's. The BL2 will be used for the yard engine while the two F's will lay over. #57 will have a cut of new Santa Fe boxcars in the evening. A considerable portion of Monon's coal traffic came from the L&N and the C&O at Louisville routed to Wisconsin Steel in Chicago via Michigan City. Freight rates in the 1950's and 1960's were structured to draw traffic to routes that were much more circuitous than those of present day. A railroad that wanted to build traffic on a particular route offered a favorable rate on traffic that was more sensitive to cost than transit time. Monon offered many such routing opportunities through out of the way junctions that by today's standards would seem odd. *(Gordon Lloyd)*

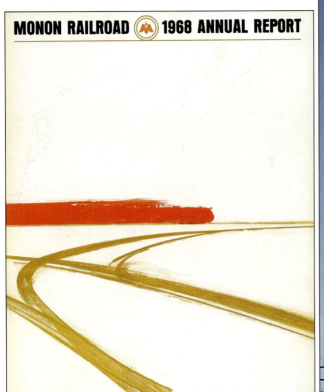

Right • RS2 56 was assigned to the Michigan City yard job on June 11, 1966. Although the BL2's dominated the Third Subdivision's assignments, the RS2's were frequent visitors. The Michigan City job received traffic with unusual routings via the South Shore that included potash from the Southwest off of the AT&SF or Pacific Northwest lumber from the C&NW or Milwaukee Road that was routed to the Erie at Wilders or the GTW at Haskells. Monon's share of the trip was only 20 or 30 miles, but the traffic provided revenue that added to the bottom line. *(Russell F. Munroe)*

Below • C628 407 pulls #56 through Haskells toward Michigan City in May of 1965. A single C628 easily handled the tonnage of the Michigan City trains. Train #56 originated in Lafayette with cars from #70 and #72. At Monon it received cars from Indianapolis brought up by #90. North of Monon it dropped off eastbound interchange cars at the Erie (Wilders), Haskells (GTW), Westville (Wabash) and Otis (NYC). In later years railroad mergers and changes in traffic patterns closed some of these interchange points. *(Robert J. Zelisko)*

LEFT • Local #49 crosses the Pennsylvania Panhandle mainline at La Crosse in October of 1949. La Crosse was one of the few locations where Monon did not interchange traffic with the line that it intersected. A small interchange of about 150 cars a year was conducted eight miles to the north at Wanatah, where the Monon crossed the Pennsylvania mainline to Philadelphia and New York. The Third Subdivision's locals, #48/49, were based at Monon and went on duty about 6:00AM daily except Sunday. The crew normally worked all of the industrial sidings and railroad interchanges as necessary, running all the way to Michigan City and return in one day. The normal power was a BL2, although other units were frequently substituted. Most of the sidings on the Michigan City line served agricultural related businesses such as grain elevators and feed mills. The Michigan City line had only six curves in its 59.6 miles. Monon had the fourth longest tangent mainline track in the USA, stretching 65 miles from Westville on the Michigan City line to Brookston on the Chicago-Louisville mainline. *(Sanford Goodrick)*

On October 18th, 1952 F3a 81B leads a football special across the GTW diamond at Haskells. Trailing behind the F units are a section Pullman, four Monon coaches, and a string of coaches borrowed from other roads. In 1952 Monon still had four heavyweight 60 series coaches to supplement the 14 streamlined coaches and 3 grill coaches that it used on the regular passenger runs. This train was received from a connecting road at Michigan City and is headed to a Purdue game in Lafayette. *(Sanford Goodrick)*

ABOVE • Monon's original mainline stretched from New Albany to Michigan City. By the late 1940's Monon ran one freight (#56/57) and one wayfreight (#48/49) each day between Monon and Michigan City. Regular passenger service had disappeared well before WWII. But Monon was quite willing to run passenger specials on the line, as it connected with every major carrier that ran east from Chicago. In October of 1949 a Notre Dame Football Special heads south through San Pierre on its way to play Purdue in West Lafayette. The consist includes a section Pullman, 5 Monon lightweight coaches, 4 C&EI heavyweight coaches, a C&EI diner and a Monon baggage car. *(Sanford Goodrick)*

French Lick Branch

Distance from Orleans	Southern Division FRENCH LICK BRANCH SEVENTH SUB-DIVISION STATIONS		Car Capacity of Siding
	ORLEANS	D Y	
7.6	7.6 Paoli		28
16.6	9.0 West Baden		
17.7	1.1 Sou...... FRENCH LICK	D Y	

BELOW • For years Monon served two plush spas at French Lick and Baden Springs in southern Indiana. It also made connections with a branch of the Southern Ry. at French Lick. The branch was short (only 17.7 miles from Orleans to French Lick) but busy. Until 1933 as many as twelve passenger trains a day ran on the branch, including trains run jointly with the Pennsylvania from Indianapolis via Gosport. After WWII a connecting train (#23 & 24) met THE BLUEGRASS at McDoel yard and carried Pullmans from Chicago to French Lick. By the time Tom Smart photographed extra 207 north at French Lick on May 2, 1965, only special passenger trains ran on the branch. Monon ran at least one Derby Special every year. At times there were as many as four or five specials. A common practice was to pick up the trains in Chicago and run them south to French Lick. The passenger could stay at one of the famous French Lick spas and then take the train to Louisville for the Derby. After the race they would return to French Lick and return to Chicago later in the evening. On May 2, 1965 the northbound Derby Special will depart at 9PM for Chicago, arriving at 7AM the next morning. The engineer was a Mr. Stephenson and the conductor was G. King. Behind coach 41 and business car 2 are seven Santa Fe *Regal* Series Pullmans and GTW business car 90. Bringing up the rear is Monon #3.

(Tom Smart, Emery Gulash collection)

MONON

The Diesel Fleet

THE HOOSIER LINE

ABOVE • Monon NW2 appears at Hammond in 1947. When Monon received its original NW2's in 1942, they were painted in solid black and bore the numbers DS1-DS3. Renumbered after the war to 11-13, they were then repainted into this attractive yellow gold and black scheme that was also used on NW2's 14-17 and the first RS2's 21-23 that were in delivered in 1947. The gold used on the freight F units and on all units delivered from mid-1947 on was distinctively more metallic in nature than this original yellow/gold. The NW2's and the RS2's in the yellow/gold scheme displayed the Hoosier Line motto in a white flowing script on the long hood together with the long red Monon herald on the cab. The first F units also displayed this herald on their noses below the lower headlight. Note that NW2 11 displays the reporting marks C.I.L., which were later replaced by MON in 1956. *(Lewis E Unnewehr)*

ABOVE • Monon owned three SW1's. The first SW1, DS 50 was delivered with NW2's 11-13 in 1942. It proved unsuitable and was sold in 1948, before the other SW1's arrived. SW1's 5 and 6 came in 1949. They were the only Monon switch engines equipped with m.u. connections. One SW1 normally was assigned to Bedford while the other unit normally ran on the New Albany switch job. Occasionally they were also used at McDoel, Indianapolis, and Lafayette. On September 4, 1963 SW1 5 sat in the Lafayette Shops. It will be sold to the Bulk Terminal Co. in 1964. *(J. David Ingles)*

RIGHT • When it was delivered to Monon in 1942, NW2 11 had the short stacks typical of early EMD switchers. Extensions were added to the stacks by 1947. By 1950 all the NW2's were repainted black and gold with the modern Monon herald in red on the cab side. Over the years heralds were added and subtracted. Some units had Monon spelled out in gold, others in white. Monon sold 11 in 1970 and EJ&E acquired it in 1972, where it served as #447. Hammond, July 4, 1965.
(K.C. Henkels, Matthew Herson collection)

RIGHT • NW2 13 sits at the Hammond engine house on July 1, 1966. In this version of the paint scheme the Monon name appears in white on the engine compartment and the front below the radiator. On an average day in the 1950's Monon needed 10 switch engines for its yard jobs. There were 7 NW2's, 2 SW1's, and an H10-44 available for these assignments. Two roadswitchers supplemented the switchers in the yards. In the 1960's the number of yard jobs was reduced and the SW1's and the H10-44 were sold, leaving the 7 NW2's to do all of the work. *(Matthew Herson)*

Left • Two years later NW2 13 sits at Belt Jct. in Indianapolis (September 2, 1968). It has been recently repainted with a black Monon on the cab. All other identification has been removed. Normally one NW2 was assigned to Indianapolis to handle the three yard jobs working out of Belt Jct. Yard. Number 13 served until the L&N merger, receiving #2203. The L&N sold it in 1982.
(Robert Yanosey collection)

Below • NW2 14 was part of a four-unit order that was delivered by EMD in early 1947. Unlike units 11-13, they had the much larger stacks that had become standard on EMD switchers after WWII. These units were also delivered in the yellow/gold scheme and were repainted black and gold by 1950. The NW2's were sturdy engines. They were occasionally used on the South Hammond to Lafayette and Michigan City locals. At McDoel they were used to push heavy freights north out of the yard. Hammond, October 14, 1967.
(Owen Leander)

Below • The rear of the cab of Monon's switcher fleet was normally painted solid black. By the mid sixties some of the units had the Monon name painted in gold. The handrails were bright yellow and the trucks were silver. Normally there were 3 NW2's at South Hammond, one at Monon, one at Indianapolis, one at Lafayette, and one at McDoel. Occasionally they were used on a local freight. Although the units were rotated between assignments they tended to stay at one location for long periods of time. NW2 14 served the Monon until 1970, when it was sold for rebuilding into EJ&E 446. Hammond, August 17, 1968.
(G. E. Lloyd)

LEFT • NW2 16 is from the second order for switchers that Monon placed in 1947. The four units in this order supplemented the first three NW2's in yard assignments. Sitting at the South Hammond engine house on June 11, 1966, 16 still displays the standard NW2 paint scheme of the 1950's with a red herald on the cab and white Monon lettering on the nose and on the hood. At one time the Hoosier Line slogan was a part of the red herald, but someone decided to paint out the slogan. Number 16 became L&N 2205 and served the L&N until 1983. *(Owen Leander)*

LEFT, CENTER • RS2 23 idles at the east side of Dearborn Station on July 10, 1965. Monon received 9 RS2's in 1947 for wayfreight and light passenger duty. One RS2 was assigned to the French Lick connection of THE BLUE GRASS (#23-34), while the others worked on local freights, usually south of Lafayette. Company records indicate that RS2's 21, 22, 24, 25, 28, and 29 were built with steam generators. Apparently the steam generator in unit 23 was added at a later point in time. *(Owen Leander)*

BELOW • In the mind of many a railfan, Monon and BL2 are synonymous. When John Barriger took over the Monon he decided to dieselize the Monon as quickly as possible. Monon had embraced the idea of the roadswitcher early, and the BL2 was EMD's early attempt at the concept. When they were new the BL2's could be found anywhere on the system, but in later years they tended to gather north of Lafayette. Although they were normally used on wayfreights and transfers, after 1960 they could be found assisting the F units on the road freights and even once in a while heading a passenger train. Photographed at Hammond on July 29, 1967, BL2 30 served from 1948 until 1970.

(K.C. Henkels, Robert Yanosey collection)

LEFT • Monon's BL2's arrived in two separate orders. Units 30-35 were built in April of 1948, while 36-38 were built in 1949. These BL2's were simple machines, having neither dynamic brakes nor steam generators. They were able to run anywhere on the system, and they were used in switching and freight service. On rare occasions they might pull a passenger train if no other passenger unit was available. Unit 36 was retired in 1970 and sold for trade in by the PRSL. Hammond, June 28, 1969. *(Owen Leander)*

LEFT AND BELOW • Monon sampled roadswitchers from three builders: Alco, EMD, and Fairbanks-Morse. Built in Beloit with 2 cycle opposed piston engine as units 36 and 37, the two H15-44's served until 1970. When they were new they were often assigned to McDoel yard and Bedford for use on the Fifth Subdivision locals. Like the BL2's and the RS2's, they could run anywhere on the railroad and were used in switching, transfer, and freight service. On this June 1966 day at Hammond H15-44 45 was being used in the yard. *(Owen Leander)*

LEFT • Battered and dirty from almost twenty years of continual use, H15-44 46 leads a wayfreight at Hammond on June 30, 1966. Ordered early in the Barriger regime, (Barriger had previously been an employee of Fairbanks-Morse), 46 was one of three Monon FM's. H10-44 18 was delivered in 1946, followed by two H15-44's in 1947. Originally #37, the H15-44 was renumbered 46 when the second order of BL2's arrived in 1949. Monon shared the maintenance headaches that many railroads experienced with FM opposed piston engines. Some roads like CNW and the Milwaukee Road learned the secrets to proper care of the FM's. Other roads disposed of the FM's in the early 60's. Monon chose to re-engine its FM's with EMD engines. There are two small stacks positioned differently than the two normal FM stacks on top of 46 that give away the fact that it no long has an FM O. P. engine inside.
(K.C. Henkels, Matthew Herson collection)

LEFT • Monon's RS2's were durable units that were well suited to the south end of the railroad. Rather than waste precious financial resources on new roadswitchers, Monon rebuilt the 9 RS2's with newer engines and traction motors in 1965 and 1966. RS2 53 began life as dual service freight and passenger unit 23 in 1947. Its steam generator stack can clearly be seen between the upper cab windows. Only a few of the RS2's carried the gold Monon herald on their cabs. 53 was frequently used on the French Lick passenger trains as well as serving as a back up unit for the 80 series F3's. It will serve the Monon until the merger with L&N and finish its career late in 1972. *(Keith Ardinger, Matthew Herson Collection)*

ABOVE • RS2 56 was one of two RS2's that never had a steam generator, thus it and RS2 57 had twice the fuel capacity of the other RS2's. Even though Monon had only 9 RS2's, there were other differences that set the units apart. Units 22 and 23 were built without M.U. connections, while 24 and 25 had Timken roller bearings. A steam generator was added to 23, while 29 had its steam generator removed in 1954. None of the RS2's had dynamic brakes. *(Owen Leander)*

Left • RS2 57 switches the yard at Hammond shortly after the L&N merger on September 22, 1971. RS2's 53, 57, and 59 received a gold Monon herald on the cab, black lettering and white safety stripes on the frames when they were repainted in the mid 1960's. The RS2's were renumbered from the 20 series to the 50 series when they were rebuilt by the Shops in 1965/66. Unit 57 was originally 27. Roller bearings were added to the RS2's before they were rebuilt into the 50 series. All of Monon's roadswitchers including the RS2's were geared for 65mph operation, as were the freight F3's. *(Owen Leander collection)*

Left • RS2's 58 and 59 were built as Alco demonstrators 1501 and 1500 in January, 1947 and sold to the Monon in August of 1947. When they were built they were essentially identical to unit 21. All of Monon's RS2's were transferred to the L&N on merger day and retired in 1972. RS2 59 is resting at South Hammond yard on September 15, 1968. *(Owen Leander)*

Right • Monon's freight F units had three distinctive black stripes around the lower headlight. When the units were delivered the old Monon rectangular herald was displayed below these stripes. When the units were repainted the herald was replaced with the Monon name in black. *(Richard Baldwin)*

Above • Monon owned a total of 24 F3a's and 6 F3b's. Ten of the F3a's were equipped for passenger service, as was one F3b (so far no one has produced a color photo of the F3b in Monon colors on a passenger train). Two of the cabs (62B and 64A) and one booster (64C) were destroyed in 1947, with locomotives of the same number replacing them. The rest of the F units remained in service until the C628's were delivered in March of 1964. The F units were renumbered in October of 1962 from the 50-80 series into the 100/200/300 series numbers. Retirement of the F3's commenced in 1964. The last recorded move of an F3b was on 73's extra south from Hammond to Lafayette on April 24, 1965. Freight F3's 101 and 108 were withdrawn from service after the first C420's were delivered in August of 1966, while passenger F3's 203, 204, 207, and 209 remained in service until at least mid-1970. 203 and 204 were transferred to the L&N and traded in to EMD in 1972. F3a 207 sits with two sister units at Hammond on June 26, 1969.

(Owen Leander)

ABOVE • Monon's first C628, 400, sits quietly at Hammond on September 22, 1964. All of Monon's Centuries were equipped with a double headlight on the front and rear of the units. The headlights had two lenses, and the larger ones had a red lens that served as an emergency light to warn oncoming trains of a problem in the event that the train lost its air or had to stop suddenly. Notice that the trucks were painted silver and the handrails are yellow. Silver trucks appeared on Monon units in October of 1960 and became a standard feature for most units. The yellow handrails appeared in late 1962. Built in 1964, 400 was traded back to Alco in 1967 for a more reliable C420. Alco sold the unit to Lehigh Valley where it became 633. *(Owen Leander)*

ABOVE • LV 636, ex-Monon 403 at Oak Island Engine Terminal, Newark, NJ in March 1975. *(Robert J. Yanosey)*

LEFT • C628 401 was at South Hammond on July 26, 1964. Delivered in March of 1964, the C628's were operated as bi-directional units and were coupled together in whatever combination that was convenient. The units were very heavy, outweighing all of the other Monon units by at least 60 tons. They were normally kept on the Chicago - Louisville and Monon – Michigan City lines. *(Owen Leander)*

LEFT • Normally two to three Monon's 628's were assigned to trains south of Lafayette, two units on train north to South Hammond, and one unit to Michigan City. Occasionally a C628 would be used on a transfer into Chicago or on a local freight. The C628's did not normally sit still very long, so their delay at the K&IT engine terminal on September 7, 1964 might be due to a need to water the units or to wait out the preparation of a train for departure later in the day.

(Tom Smart, Matthew Herson collection)

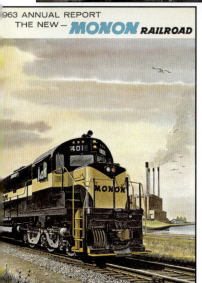

ABOVE • In 1963, a confident Monon ordered 9 C628's to power coal trains from the Ohio River to a Lake Michigan transfer port that was never built. Used instead to replace F units on freights #70-73, two C628's could pull up to 150 cars almost anywhere north of Bainbridge. South of Bainbridge was another matter, and it was common to use 3 C628's together. Unfortunately, the C628's were not well suited to Monon's needs. They were hard on the track and could not be used on the Indianapolis line. In 1967 Monon sent the C628's back to Alco in trade for 12 smaller, more versatile C420's. Hammond Ind, June 11, 1964.

(Robert C. Anderson, Matthew Herson collection)

BELOW • C628 408 and 405 sit at South Hammond later in their career. In normal operation the C628's were exchanged at Lafayette or the engine consist was reduced from three to two units for operation north of Lafayette. Since the 70 series freights normally were reblocked or exchanged cuts of cars at Shops Yard, the hostlers usually had one or two hours to service units running through or to cut units in or out of a consist. The large fuel tanks of the C628's enabled them to make several trips between refueling. *(Owen Leander)*

ABOVE • Monon's two passenger C420's were quite sufficient for the motive power needs of #5 & #6. Since one unit powered the trains for about a week at a time, the other was freely mixed with the other C420's and run wherever it was needed and the C420's could run anywhere on the railroad. C420 501 made its maiden run on the Monon on Tuesday August 30, 1966 when it powered a passenger extra made up of coach 25 and business car 1 from Lafayette to Louisville that included a side trip down the Midland branch. The next day it powered the special from Louisville to Bloomington. Four months later it was serviced together with RS2 56 and C628 407 at Youngstown on December 18, 1966.

(Tom Smart, Matthew Herson collection)

ABOVE • Brand new C420's 505 and 504 have just arrived with #73 at Youngstown yard on their maiden voyage on August 22, 1966. They left Shops Yard together with C628's 403 and 401 at 9:10AM and arrived at 4:50PM. The power set was turned north to Lafayette on #70 that evening at 6:50PM. On the 23rd 504 again ran on #73/70 while 505 remained at the Shops. On the 24th 505 led #71 south from Shops while 504 took a turn on #6 to Chicago, returning on #5 (even though it did not have a steam generator for passenger service). On the 25th 505 was combined with 503 running an extra to South Hammond and back.

(Tom Smart, Matthew Herson collection)

ABOVE • C420 506 sits at Binghamton, N.Y. waiting to be delivered to the Monon. The C420's were delivered slightly out of order. Monon tested the units in different assignments as they were delivered. C420 503 arrived the week of August 15, 1966 ahead of its sister units. It spent much of its time running on the locals between Lafayette and McDoel. 504 and 505 arrived next and were assigned to freight service. 506 was placed in service on Friday August 26, 1966, making its first run south on #71 to Youngstown. The first passenger C420, 501, was placed in service on the 30th, with 502 following shortly behind it. *(Edward Lewnard collection)*

BELOW • Monon learned an important lesson about its motive power requirements from the limitations that it experienced with the C628's. When the C420's were ordered the railroad was looking for modestly sized, flexible units that could go anywhere on the railroad and perform any task. The Monon found its ideal locomotive in the C420. To enhance the C420's flexibility they were built with dual controls at an added expense of $3800 per unit and a Mars rotating signal light with red and white lenses above the headlight on the rear as well as the front of the unit. Surprisingly, none of the C420's was equipped with dynamic brakes, even though the engineers on the south end of the railroad could have put them to good use. C420 #510 sit between runs at South Hammond on October 10, 1970. *(Owen Leander collection)*

RIGHT • One distinguishing feature that made the Monon C420's unique was the large bell that was placed on the short hood in front of the cab. As was standard practice by the time they were delivered, the engines from #70 were split up at South Hammond in the morning. One unit might be used as a yard switcher while the others would take the BRC transfer north later in the morning. C420 512 sits on the yard lead near the freight house, pausing between switch moves on July 3, 1971. *(James Lewnard)*

Above • C420 512 sits with U23b 607 at South Hammond in the late afternoon of May 15, 1971. 512 was part of a twelve-unit order for C420's delivered August of 1967, one year after the original C420's arrived on the property. They immediately replaced the nine C628's, which were traded back to Alco and were resold to the Lehigh Valley. The two groups of C420's were essentially identical. Like the C628's, the C420's were equipped with double headlights that included a red lens on both ends. Monon also found that the long, low nose at the front of the C420 was ideal place to display a large locomotive bell that would do justice to a steam engine. None of Monon's C420 was equipped with dynamic brakes. Weighing in at 272,000 pounds, the C420 were geared for 70 mph, had fuel tanks that held 3100 gallons of fuel, and displayed Nathan five chime horns. The original specifications required that the trucks be interchangeable with the trucks used on the RS2's and that the cabs be equipped with dual controls.
(Owen Leander)

Right, Center • Shortly after the merger with the L&N C420's 515 and 504 pull back into South Hammond Yard. All of Monon's C420's were transferred to the L&N at the time of the merger where they remained in service until at least 1979. The majority of the units were retired in 1982. At least seven of the C420's served on other railroads after the L&N set them aside. On the L&N 515 received the number 1332. Later it was sold to the Indiana Hi-Rail where it carried the number 332.
(Owen Leander collection)

Right • Unfortunately for the Monon, Alco did not receive enough orders to stay in business, so the next time Monon needed diesels it had to order from General Electric if it didn't wish to go back to EMD. GE had never offered a unit as small as the C420 so Monon ordered eight U23b's to supplement the C420's. By this time the few remaining F3's and BL2's were completely worn out, and the rebuilt RS2's were beginning to show their age. Three nearly new U23b's sit next to the mainline at the north end of South Hammond Yard in April of 1970.
(Alfred Jones, John Hanacek collection)

Above • The U23b's were delivered with different color gold than all of the previous units Monon operated. The units were 6 tons heavier than the C420's and had 300 more horsepower, but for all intents and purposes they were used in the same roles that the C420's functioned in. On May 15, 1971 U23b 601 prepares to take a transfer into Chicago from South Hammond. *(Owen Leander)*

Above • U23b's 604 and 606 sit between runs at South Hammond on October 10, 1970. Three U23b's were sufficient to handle most freights on the north end of the Monon, while four units were standard on the south end. The U23b's arrived 15 months before the L&N merger took place. By late 1970 it was possible to run all of the road freights with the C420's and the U23b's. The RS2's ran the locals and helped the remaining NW2's in the yards.
(Owen Leander)

Below • U23B 608 and 605 make up a second set of units at South Hammond on October 10, 1970. In the year before the U23b's arrived the Monon freights were totally entrusted to the C420's and the RS2's, as there were only 3 F3's left in service. It was common for two U23b's to power a transfer into Chicago, although they had enough power so that only one unit might be needed.
(Owen Leander)

MONON
THE HOOSIER LINE

The Freight Car Fleet

ABOVE • Every railroad has miscellaneous cars that are assigned to special duties and are in many ways unique to that railroad. One of Monon's most unique cars was triple dome tank car 1805, which was assigned to the stores department at Lafayette. The car had a 40-ton capacity. The dome on the right says that it is dedicated to car oil, while the dome on the left says fortnite oil. The data on the side says the car was released from Shops in December 1954, and that it was last serviced at Lafayette on April 26, 1963. *(Richard Baldwin)*

ABOVE • Monon 40' box cars 276 and 887 stand on the Milwaukee Road mainline at Othello, Washington on May 31, 1963. When John Barriger became the president of the Monon in 1946 the road was worn out from heavy wartime traffic. Its freight car fleet was ancient and decrepit. There were only 420 modern steel boxcars available for service. In June of 1947 Monon acquired 500 40' steel boxcars from Pullman-Standard. These cars were pre-PS1 boxcars with Dreadnought ends and Murphy steel roofs. Cars 501-533 built in 1949 were PS1 box cars. Cars 1-250 had Superior doors while cars 251-500 had Camel doors. *(Wade Stevenson)*

Above ◉ In the years following WWII Monon gradually added new cars to its box car fleet so that by 1957 it had placed 1,385 40ft. boxcars in service. Pullman-Standard built 130 PS1 box cars numbered 865-994 in April of 1957. Delivered in the then current Hoosier Line paint scheme, the cars were painted box car red with a light grayish white band at the top proclaiming The Hoosier Line in black. The ends and underbody were black, while all other lettering was displayed in white. The cars were equipped with 6-foot wide corrugated doors and Pullman-Standard's unique end. Car 916 appeared at Kankakee on June 29, 1977 still displaying its original paint scheme. *(James Lewnard)*

Above ◉ Monon 50 ft double door box car 1508 rolls through Deval interlocking in Des Plaines, Illinois on August 6, 1975 in a much simplified Monon paint scheme. Fifty cars numbered 1501-1550 were built by Pressed Steel Car Co. in April of 1948, but by 1951 there were only three cars left in the series. Monon equipped many of its 50-ft cars with special loading devices and renumbered the cars into different number blocks to indicate the service they were assigned to. *(James Lewnard)*

ABOVE • Brand new 50ft double door box 1271 sits at Lafayette Shops on May 16, 1948 awaiting its first assignment. Painted in solid boxcar red, it has the double teepee Hoosier Line herald and white lettering. *(E. Van Dusen)*

ABOVE • Monon 50-ft double door box 1521 was part of a series of cars built in 1948 that was renumbered when the cars were assigned to special services. Some of the cars were renumbered back in the 1500 series in the 1960's. *(Paul C. Winters)*

ABOVE • When the Depression eased just before the beginning of WWII Monon was desperately in need of new cars. In 1941 Pullman-Standard built 150 cars numbered 9000-9149 and in 1942 added another 300 cars numbered 9150- 9449. They were painted in boxcar red with white lettering and the reliable service herald of the Chicago, Indianapolis, and Louisville. The cars had riveted sides, dreadnaught ends, and 7 panel superior doors. Shortly after WWII 25 of the cars were rebuilt with Evans loading devices, renumbered 1201-1225, and repainted into a solid gray scheme with red lettering. In the 1960's the remaining cars were rebuilt by Lafayette Shops and renumbered beginning with 9500. Box cars 9635 and 9637 appear together in the standard 1960 era paint with a large Monon on the left and a simplified herald on the right.

(Paul C. Winters)

ABOVE • Monon hauled a considerable amount of grain and assigned a large numbers of boxcars to this service. To assist in the loading the cars round grain hatches were added to many of Monon's 40ft and 50ft cars in the 1960's. Rebuilt from a 1-500 series car, box car 10330 follows a BRC SW1500 into CNW's Proviso Yard in August of 1979. *(James Lewnard)*

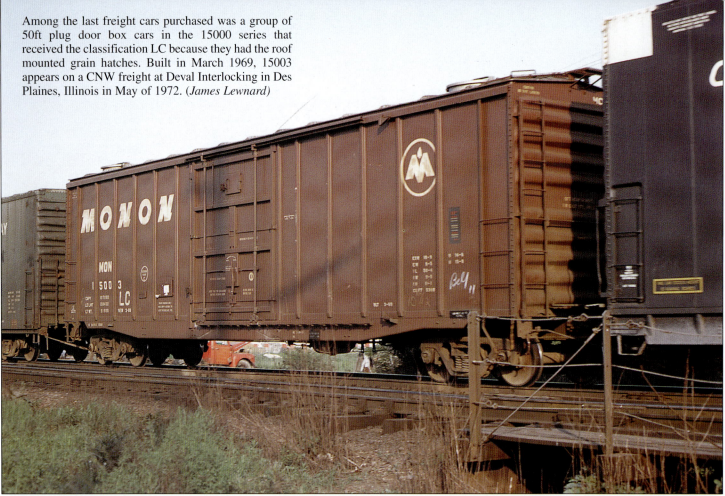

Among the last freight cars purchased was a group of 50ft plug door box cars in the 15000 series that received the classification LC because they had the roof mounted grain hatches. Built in March 1969, 15003 appears on a CNW freight at Deval Interlocking in Des Plaines, Illinois in May of 1972. *(James Lewnard)*

Above • Monon maintained a small fleet of low-sided gondolas rebuilt from flat cars that were used for hauling steel and pipe. Gondola 35041 was built in 1952 and was assigned to the EJ&E at Gary for steel loading. *(Paul C. Winters)*

Below • Forty foot covered hopper 56005 was assigned to stone dust service on the L&N at Gantts Jct., Alabama when it appeared at Kankakee in January of 1977. Originally built in 1947, it has been renewed and renumbered by the Lafayette Shops. *(James Lewnard)*

ABOVE • One of the few groups of cars retained by the Monon after WWII that were built in the 1920's was a group of 250 wood sided two bay hopper cars in series 40000-40249. Built by Pullman in 1925, the cars were renewed and kept in service into the 1960's. Hopper cars 40102 and 40205 appear at Monon on December 28, 1963 in the contemporary paint scheme with white lettering and Hoosier Line heralds. *(George Berisso)*

ABOVE • For years Monon hoppers had been painted boxcar red with white lettering. But in 1957, someone at Shops decided that the hoppers would be far more attractive if they were painted black with gold lettering. The same stencils for the herald and the speed lettering were used with different colors being applied. Two bay hopper 41501 was one of the first steel Monon hoppers constructed in September of 1940. Fort Wayne, Indiana. *(Emery Gulash, Robert Yanosey collection)*

ABOVE • When the 41500 series 2 bay hoppers were delivered to the Monon in 1940, they were among the first news cars received by the bankrupt carrier since the Great Crash of the stock market in 1929. The Monon would never have been able to operate during WWII without these cars. Pullman built 100 cars in series 41500 to 41599 with New York air brakes and 100 cars in series 41600 to 41699 with Westinghouse air brakes. Over the years they carried at least five variations of the Monon paint scheme. Weighing in at just about 19 tons each, they carried up to 50 tons of coal or stone. Monon also had a similar series of 2 bay hoppers built by Pullman-Standard in 1954 numbered 4001-4150. In the early sixties, many of the 41500 series cars wore out their sides, and they were rebuilt with new side sheets and side braces, totally changing their outward appearance. Ft. Wayne.
(Emery Gulash, Robert Yanosey collection)

ABOVE • Hopper 41576 was renewed in November of 1957 and repainted in the then current black and gold scheme. It is coupled to rider caboose 81225 in January 1958.
(John Hanacek collection)

LEFT • The 41000 series 34' two bay hoppers were rebuilt by the Monon in the 1960's with ribbed sides to extend their service lives. Many of them remained in service at the time of the L&N merger. *(Copyright J. W. Smith, 2000, used with permission)*

ABOVE • Like many railroads Monon relied upon the Fruit Growers Express Company to provide insulated boxcars and refrigerators for its special shipment needs. Insulated Box car 90261 was part of a small group of cars assigned to the Monon in the 1970's. It was assigned to a pool of cars that the Milwaukee Road provided to the Johnson's Wax Company at Waxdale, Wisconsin, near Racine., where it was frequently loaded with household cleaning supplies. Kankakee, March 6, 1977. *(James Lewnard)*

ABOVE • On November 18, 1979 a mixed group of Monon and CNW covered hoppers move through CNW's Proviso yard on a transfer, including 50025, one of Monon's most modern covered hoppers. These cars were assigned to cement service at Mitchell, Indiana and could be found throughout the nation, serving the L&N long after the merger with the Monon. *(James Lewnard)*

MONON
The Passenger Car Fleet
The Hoosier Line

ABOVE • Business Car 1 sits on a sidetrack near the turntable at the South Hammond round house on May 3, 1963. Built in 1925, number 1 was acquired in 1946 from the Tennessee Central where she wore the number 100. Number 1 had a complete kitchen and dining room, two staterooms, a section room, and an observation room. Shortly after this picture was taken number 1 was sold to the Green Bay Railway Museum, where it can still be seen today, although she it is no longer painted red and gray. For several years after its acquisition number 1 was used for excursions to Chicago, appearing occasionally in the CNW coach yards laying over between runs. *(K.C. Henkels, collection of Robert Yanosey)*

ABOVE • Making a pre-Christmas trip at Pekin on December 20, 1957, *Lynne* brings up the rear of #6. *Lynne* served the Monon until it was sold to Brown Inc. in the late 1960's. It was restored in 1987 and is still used as a private car in passenger service.
(Lloyd Kimble, Michael Sink collection)

116

ABOVE • The late afternoon sun shines on the rear platform of business car #2, which also bore the name *Lynne*. Originally built by the Pullman Co. in 1925, *Lynne* was rebuilt by the Monon in April 1954 to serve as the railroad's premier business car. *Lynne* had a kitchen, dining room, a drawing room, two compartments and a large observation room. Finished in red and gray and later repainted in black and gold, *Lynne* was used by the president of the Monon to entertain guests as well as to make inspection trips over the railroad. Dearborn Station, March 1959. (Richard Baldwin)

Above • In the years after WWII Monon maintained a small fleet of railway postal cars with 30' mailrooms for sorting the mail and a baggage room for checked baggage and express shipments. Cars 17 and 18 were 63' cars built in 1913. RPO 17 was previously numbered 508 and 18 was 512. Both were painted red and gray for service on #5/6. Car 17 was retired before 1952 and car 18 was retired in 1953. Cars 11 and 12 were rebuilt in 1947 from Army hospital cars that were originally constructed in 1944. They normally served on #11-15 to Indianapolis until those trains were discontinued. Both 11 and 12 were painted red and gray for their entire service lives. RPO cars 13,14, and 19 were converted from 74' baggage cars 431, 432 and 435 in the late 1940's for service on Louisville trains #5/6, although they were also used on #11-15 when needed. These three RPO's were also painted red and gray, but were repainted black and gold beginning in 1961. They provided postal service on #5/6 until the Post Office discontinued the routes in December 1965. For the remaining years of passenger service they were used for baggage and express service. RPO 19 trails RS2 55 on train #6 at Dearborn Station on September 16, 1967. *(Owen Leander)*

Above • When John Barriger became the president of the Monon the railroad's newest coaches were four round roof heavyweight cars numbered 61 to 64, built in 1923 by Pullman. One of the first projects Barriger initiated was the construction of two complete streamliners rebuilt from Army hospital cars in 1947. Six coaches, numbered 21-26, entered service on THE HOOSIER and THE TIPPECANOE. Painted in a an attractive light gray, red, and medium gray paint scheme, the cars seated 46 passengers in the main room with 5 more seats available in the smoking lounge. These cars served as a group until 1959 after Monon had discontinued the Indianapolis trains. Beginning in 1959 three of the 20 series coaches were rebuilt into cars 43-45 until only coach 25 and 26 were left. Coach 26 was retired in late 1964 or 1965. All of the remaining coaches were repainted in black and gold. Coach 25 stayed in service until THE THOROUGHBRED was discontinued in September of 1967. It appears at the 51st St. coach yards in Chicago on May 13, 1967. *(Owen Leander)*

ABOVE • Monon added eight more streamlined coaches in 1948, numbered 27-34. Although similar in most respects to cars 21-26, they had a different window arrangement and a slightly different interior. These coaches were also delivered in the red and gray paint scheme. Apparently only coach 34 was repainted in black and gold. The 27-34 series served from 1948 until 1960, when 7 of the coaches were retired, leaving car 34 in service. It is believed that coach 34 was rebuilt into coach 46 in 1965. On October 16, 1956 four Monon coaches and two diners sit in the CUT coach yard in Cincinnati, Ohio, laying over from a special train. Coach 28 and the other cars all display the modified red/gray paint scheme, with the letterboard repainted with the darker gray and the roof painted black. Note that all of Monon's streamlined cars had six wheel trucks. *(Lou Schmitz)*

RIGHT AND BELOW • Coach 41 was rebuilt from grille coach 65 in May of 1956. Monon built three grille coaches (65-67) in 1948 to supplement the three dining cars (51-53) and 2 diner-parlor observations (58-59). They were used on special moves, college trains, and on #5/6 after the diner parlor cars were discontinued. When coach 41 was constructed the grille section was stripped from the interior and the car was reconfigured with 70 seats. The smoking lounge was taken out and the men's restroom became the women's restroom. A smaller men's restroom was added at the opposite end of the car where the grille section had been. At a later point in time the air conditioning system was changed from an ice system to an electromechanical system. The prominent grille in the middle of the car near the vestibule indicates that the car has the more modern air conditioning system. *(Owen Leander, right; Paul C. Winters, below)*

Above • Monon coach 42 was reconstructed from coach 29 with an expanded seating capacity of 75. Although the interior of car 42 resembled that of 41, it had a group of seven small seats next to the women's restroom. Car 43 was reconstructed from coach 21 with an interior similar to that of 42. Apparently coaches 42 and 43 were the last cars painted in the gray and red scheme, as the other coaches and headend cars began to be repainted into black and gold shortly after 42 and 43 re-entered service. Lafayette, June 1961. (*Edward Lewnard collection*)

Above • Coach 45 sits on a sidetrack at the south end of Dearborn Station on June 11, 1967. It was rebuilt from a 20 series coach in late 1964 with a new air conditioning system and 73 seats. Note that the black and gold coaches had a red and gold herald in the center of the car side. (*Owen Leander*)

RIGHT • Coach 46, the last Monon rebuilt coach by the Shops, trails another 40 series coach and a baggage car on #6 at Hammond in August of 1967. Apparently it was reconstructed from coach 34 in 1965. It also had seating for 73 persons. *(Alfred Jones, John Hanacek collection)*

BELOW • After WWII most of Monon's headend cars were ancient relics built before WWI. At the end of the war Monon acquired a group of Pullman tourist sleepers that intended to convert to other useful purposes. Four of the tourist cars were rebuilt into baggage cars. The first and most distinctive of these cars was 101, which had a unique, streamlined roof, unlike the other three baggage cars, which had celestory roofs. Originally built as a 1 drawing room, 1 bedroom, observation lounge named *Huron Valley*, it was rebuilt into tourist car 6080 in 1943. Rebuilt and released by Shops in November 1947, it was most frequently used on #5/6 in both storage mail and baggage/express service. 101 remained in service until the passenger trains were discontinued on September 30, 1967. *(Owen Leander)*

BELOW • Baggage car 102 is loaded with mail and express at Dearborn Station on July 10, 1965. Monon had three baggage cars rebuilt from tourist sleepers that resembled each other (102-104), but yet each car had a distinctive arrangement of its doors that it apart from the other two cars. Built as 26-seat drawing room parlor car named *Louise*, it was rebuilt by Pullman into Tourist car 6004 in August 1942. Monon converted 6004 into 102 in November 1947. All of these cars were originally painted red and gray, and all of them (101-104) were repainted black and gold in the early 1960's. *(Owen Leander)*

ABOVE • At the beginning of WWII Monon's need for baggage cars was so great that it acquired 7 heavyweight cars from St. Louis Car Co. in March 1942 (430-436). Painted in Pullman green with gold lettering, they were used on all of Monon's passenger trains. Three of these cars were rebuilt into 30' RPO baggage cars 13, 14, and 19 in the late 1940's. The remaining four cars were renumbered 106-109. They retained their four-wheel trucks and were repainted into red and gray. Baggage car 106 sits just south of the Roosevelt Rd. bridge at Dearborn Station on June 11, 1967, waiting to be placed into proper position for its departure on #5 in the evening. It as repainted black and gold in the early 1960's, and will be used until the end of passenger service in September of 1967. *(Owen Leander)*

ABOVE • Perhaps the last Monon passenger car to retain the red and gray colors, baggage car 108 sits behind the Lafayette Shops in January 1972. When passenger service was discontinued most of the passenger cars were brought to Lafayette. Some of them were converted to work train service, while the rest waited our their days sitting in the back yard. Note that the car retained its four-wheel friction bearing trucks until the end. *(copyright J.W. Smith, used with permission)*

RIGHT • In the years following WWI Monon rarely had money for new equipment, especially for head end cars. By 1942 much of its older wooden car fleet was completely worn out. So Monon splurged, buying seven heavyweight baggage cars. Four of these cars were repainted and renumbered when the new coaches were introduced in 1947. Baggage car 109 was built by the St. Louis Car Co. as 436. It was one of the last cars in red and gray paint. Dearborn Station, December 28, 1963. *(George Berisso)*

ABOVE ◦ A handful of Monon's aging heavyweight cars remained in service after the streamlined cars were built in 1947-48. Barney and Smith built baggage coach 317 in 1912 together with its sister car 316. The double baggage doors on each side of the car were a distinctive trait of the Monon baggage coaches. There were 32 seats for passengers in its coach section. One of the last regular assignments for 317 was the French Lick trains #23/24 that connected with trains #3/4, THE BLUEGRASS, at Bloomington. A common consist of #24/24 would be an RS2, 317, and one of Monon's four 10-1-2 Pullman cars in Chicago to French Lick service. (Monon never owned a streamlined Pullman, but it did borrow many Pullmans for special train movements, such as the Kentucky Derby Specials). When the Monon depot was destroyed in the tragic wreck of September 17, 1951, 317 was brought to the junction, taken off of its trucks, and set in place to be used as a temporary depot. *(J. Schmidt, Owen Leander collection)*

LEFT ◦ In the mid 1950's Monon's management made a concerted effort capture more head end business for the three remaining passenger runs, (two to Indianapolis and one to Louisville), The eight existing baggage cars were clearly insufficient for the traffic, so Monon refitted six regular box cars with steam lines and signals for passenger service. Even these cars were not sufficient so in 1954 Monon rebuilt eight former U.S. army kitchen cars into express cars. Numbered 2203 through 2210, they were originally painted red and gray. Express cars 2204 and 2208 trail F3a 82a as THE THOROUGHBRED departs Lafayette Shops for Chicago on August 10, 1958. *(Richard Baldwin)*

RIGHT ◦ Express car 2210 sits at the Monon depot in Lafayette on July 5, 1968. Cars 2205-2210 remained in service until passenger trains were discontinued in 1967. They were all repainted black and gold. When the troop kitchens were built in 1944 they were equipped with a cushioned truck manufactured by the Allied Railway Equipment Co. These trucks proved unstable in service, and many railroads replaced them with a different design. 2210 thus has replacement trucks. Monon also rebuilt another troop kitchen car into heater car X5, which was later renumbered 2200. *(James Lewnard)*

MONON
The Hoosier Line

Cabooses and Work Equipment

ABOVE • Monon had a large fleet of steel underframe wood bodied cabooses built by American Car and Foundry in 1929. They were the backbone of Monon's caboose fleet until the first steel cabooses were built in 1952. The wood cars were used in all types of freight service, being gradually downgraded to assignments on transfers and work trains. The remaining cars were renumbered 81301-81314 at the same time that the new steel cabooses were renumbered into the 81500 series. Caboose 80010 was again renumbered from an 81300 series car when it was placed in work train service. It sits quietly with other work cars at South Hammond on October 14, 1967. *(Owen Leander)*

RIGHT • Another wood cupola caboose sits at South Hammond on January 15, 1967, its number almost unreadable to the flaking of its paint. Many of these wooden cabooses remained in local service in the early 1960's until gradually replaced by Monon's homebuilt extended vision cabooses. The Monon Historical Society recently completed the restoration of caboose C287, which is now displayed next to the former Monon/NKP depot at Linden. The Kentucky Railway Museum also has car C302. *(Owen Leander)*

RIGHT • In early 1946 Monon decided to renew its fleet of wooden cupola cabooses by rebuilding them with steel bay windows. By 1948 at least fifteen of these cars were rebuilt. The cars retained their original 200-300 series numbers when they were rebuilt. When John Barriger became president several of the wooden cabooses were repainted a bright red with black roofs and bold white lettering. Like the other wooden cars the bay window cabooses were renumbered together into a common numbers series as 81401-81412. Then in the early 60's some of the cars were relegated to work train service, repainted in maintenance colors, and again renumbered. The cars finished their service by 1970. Caboose 80011, labeled the Indian Trail Motel by a local admirer, sits at South Hammond on August 14, 1967. *(Owen Leander)*

124

Right • Perhaps the most distinctive cars in Monon's fleet were the head end cabooses that were used on the many locals that ran across the system. Built on the frames of eight stone gondolas, four cars were constructed in 1945/46. (#C211-C214, later renumbered 81211-81214) and four were constructed in 1956 (#81222-81225). One car was constructed for each of the eight local trains Monon ran at the time. Each car had a 16' crew compartment and a 22' baggage compartment, which was used to handle less than carload shipments at the many rural stations served by the Monon. Note that there is a back-up light on the end of the car. Normally the ran right behind the diesels, but occasionally they ran at the end of a train. October, 1964. *(Richard Baldwin)*

Right • When WWII ended the Monon's rolling stock was in sad shape. As new steel freight cars were added to the fleet, large numbers of wood cars disappeared. The one exception was the wood cabooses. Since they were in reasonably good shape, at least twelve were rebuilt with steel bay windows. Many of them were painted bright red. The cupolas were removed from another group of seven cars, but they did not receive bay windows. The bay window cars became 81401-81412 while the flat top cars became 81101-81107. As the steel cabooses were delivered the wood cars were relegated to work train service. A surprising number of these wooden cabooses were sold to local farmers and businesses. Renumbered 81402, one of the last wood cars, sits behind Lafayette Shops in July of 1968. *(James Lewnard)*

Below • Although Monon spent a fortune purchasing new diesels and freight cars to rebuild the railroad after WWII, no new cabooses were ordered until 1952. In September Thrall delivered a one of a kind steel cupola caboose C350 with an off-center cupola. Then in December the International Car Company delivered nine steel cupola cabooses numbered C360-C368. Renumbered 81501-81509 three years later, they served until the merger with the L&N in 1971. When the cars were built, the Monon name was displayed in medium sized lettering with the herald between the two side windows. In later years the Monon lettering was enlarged and placed on the lower portion of the car side, while a smaller herald was centered between the two windows. South Hammond, October 10, 1970. *(Owen Leander)*

LEFT • For a small railroad Monon had a tremendous variety of cabooses. The original International cabooses in the 81500 series were well suited to the Monon's needs. They closely resembled cars built for several other eastern roads at the time. When they were originally built the platforms, handrails and lettering was done in silver, but in later years this was changed to white. Caboose 81506 sits at South Hammond in the mid 1960's.
(Joseph Lewnard collection)

ABOVE • In 1956 Monon decided to build eight steel cabooses to its own design in the Lafayette Shops. Although they were similar to the International cabooses built in 1952, they had several features unique to the Monon. First, cabooses 81525 to 81532 had welded rather than riveted construction. Second, they had extended bay windows attached to the cupolas. Third, they had two large curved windows each side rather than the more common square pointed rectangular windows of their predecessors. Caboose 81526 trails a freight at Hammond on June 11, 1966. *(Russell Munroe)*

BELOW • In a comprehensive article on the 81525 series cabooses that appeared in *The Hoosier Line* of April 1985 Mont Switzer determined that Monon painted these cabooses in six variations of the red and black paint scheme. On August 28, 1971 caboose 81528 sits at South Hammond. The sides are red, the roof and underframe are black, the platforms and safety equipment are silver, and the lettering is white. *(James Lewnard)*

RIGHT, TOP • The cupolas of Monon's newest cabooses had a distinct peak that sets them apart from other similar cabooses built to similar designs for other railroads. Together with the 81500 series, the 81525 cars provided for most of Monon's needs until the merger with the L&N. All of the steel cabooses were transferred to the L&N where they continued to serve until the advent of rear-end devices in the 1980's.
(Owen Leander)

RIGHT, CENTER • In an age in which a caboose was considered a necessity any time a train left the yards, Monon needed inexpensive cars that could provide the rear end crew with the basic equipment needed to operate the transfers into Chicago. Although road cabooses could be used on transfers, for many years the older wooden cars were assigned to these less demanding tasks. When the wood cabooses wore out, Monon built the 81551 series cabooses. With two large platforms at either end and no cupola, these cars were well suited to the task. Caboose 81552 is at South Hammond in May of 1967.
(John Kuehl, Joseph Lewnard collection)

BELOW • Monon constructed three transfer cabooses at Shops in 1959. They were numbered 81551-81553 and were originally painted red and black with white lettering. At some point in the mid 1960's 81552 was repainted boxcar red. It spent much of its time in transfer service operating from South Hammond to the yards of Monon's connecting railroads. On July 3, 1971 the conductor and brakeman enjoy the warmth of a late summer afternoon as their transfer returns to South Hammond. Note that they have provided themselves with an extra chair on the front platform, perhaps to read the newspaper as the train made its leisurely journey through the city of Chicago.
(James Lewnard)

RIGHT, TOP • One of the most unusual cars on the Monon roster was bunk car 80057. Rebuilt from an ancient passenger car, it sits at South Hammond on a work train on October 14, 1967. *(Owen Leander)*

RIGHT, CENTER • Express car 80066 has received freight car trucks and been downgraded to work train service. Several of the express cars were used for company service after the passenger trains were discontinued and the L&N used them after the merger with the Monon.
(Owen Leander)

BELOW • When the Pullman company was divided into two separate corporations following WWII, the railroads that operated Pullman cars on their trains were given the ownership of the majority of the sleeping cars then in operation. The Pullman company retained a sizeable fleet of heavyweight cars for pool service, while most of the lightweight and many of the heavyweight cars were transferred to railroads. Monon received four 10 section, 1 drawing room, two compartment cars which it used on Chicago-French Lick/Louisville trains 2/3, THE BLUEGRASS. When THE BLUEGRASS was discontinued. the Monon sleeping cars continued to be used in the Pullman pool. Gradually they were withdrawn from Pullman lease and converted to work train service. Ten section Pullman 80151 is either the former *Camp Meigs* or *Camp Dix*, (company records are not clear - one car became 80151 and the other 80178). Camp car 80151 sits at South Hammond on August 14, 1967 in work train service. *(Owen Leander)*

RIGHT • Monon purchased a total of 14 tourist Pullmans in September of 1947. Four of these cars were converted to baggage cars while eight of them were turned into camp cars. Car 80166 was originally a 12 section, 1 drawing room Pullman named *Weedsport*, which the Pullman company converted into tourist car 2528 in March 1943. South Hammond, January 1, 1966.
(Owen Leander)